# AA-1025

The Memoirs of
an Anti-Apostle

# AA-1025

## The Memoirs of an Anti-Apostle

*by*

Marie Carré

TAN BOOKS AND PUBLISHERS, INC.
Rockford, Illinois 61105

This book was originally published in May, 1972 in French under the title *ES-1025* by Editions Segieb, 78 Freneuse, France.

The English edition of this book was originally published in 1973 by Éditions Saint-Raphaël, 31, rue King Quest, suite 212, Sherbrooke, Quebec, Canada.

This English edition copyright © 1991 by TAN Books and Publishers, Inc.

Library of Congress Catalog Card No:   91-75254

ISBN:   0-89555-449-6

Printed and bound in the United States of America.

TAN BOOKS AND PUBLISHERS, INC.
P.O. Box 424
Rockford, Illinois 61105

1991

## *Notice*
## *From The French Edition*

This book is a dramatized presentation of certain facts which are occurring in the Church and which are perplexing to many of the faithful.

All resemblance to persons or contemporary events are not to be considered as purely accidental.

## *Testimony*

It has been my privilege and pleasure to read three times the book written by Marie Carré, and whose French title is *ES 1025* and to compare it, line after line, with this English translation.

Therefore, I do hereby certify that this translation is accurate and gives the English reader a genuine knowledge of the contents of this valuable book. I also feel that it is my Christian duty to invite English-speaking Catholics to read this book if they wish to understand clearly what His Holiness Pope Paul VI meant when he warned Catholics not to participate in the "auto-demolition" of their Church, that is, its destruction "from within." This reading will remind Catholics of their duty of faithfulness and devotedness towards their Church and its Chief, the Pope of Rome.

—Rev. Ira J. Bourassa,
D.P., B.A., D.Ph., D.Th.

## *Publisher's Note About This Book*

Marie Carré was a French nurse and a convert from Protestantism in 1965. She died in Marseille, France in 1984. In May, 1972 she had *AA-1025* published by Editions Segieb in Freneuse, France under the title *ES-1025*, which stands for *Élève Seminariste – 1025*, or "Seminary Student–1025." In 1973 the book was published in both French and English by Éditions Saint-Raphaël in Sherbrooke, Quebec, Canada, the English edition of which had been printed seven times by 1988.

According to the publisher at Éditions Saint-Raphaël, the story as she tells it is essentially true and the way it happened; however, she did, apparently, do some slight editing of the text to make it more readable. Nonetheless, there is obviously a strong difference in style between Marie Carré's Prologue and her interjected editorial comment on pages 94 to 98, on the one hand, and the text itself, on the other, which is strong indication that the story was written by someone else. Also, there is evidence of authenticity in the Memoirs themselves, which discuss a matter that did not take place until approximately 1980 to 1983, namely, the adulation given to Martin Luther in various quarters in the Church—this especially leading up to the 500th centennial of his birth in 1983. It is not reasonable to imagine that a nurse, or anyone else, for that matter, could have predicted in 1971 or 1972 that various people in the Catholic Church would, within ten years, be extolling Martin Luther as some sort of religious hero.

Even if this book were pure fabrication from beginning to end, nonetheless, what it claims to prognosticate has actually come true—unerringly so! Besides this, moreover, all the many profound and even revolutionary changes that have occurred within the Catholic Church since Vatican Council II (1962-1965) had to have been conceived in the minds of people intimately familiar with the workings of the Catholic Church and also had to have been promoted by such people through influential channels *within* the Church, or they would never have been accepted and put into place.

*AA-1025* makes profoundly thought-provoking reading today, when we in our time have seen virtually all the changes discussed in this book come to pass.

# *Prologue*

How must one begin to write a book when not a writer, or rather, how can one explain that he believes it is his duty to publish memoirs— memoirs that are quite terrible (and precisely because they are so terribly disquieting)?

Then, let us say that these first pages are an appeal to Catholics of today in the form of a fore-word or rather a confession. Yes, "a confession" (insofar as "poor little me" is concerned) seems to be the right word, although it is one of those words which no one wishes to use nowadays. Well, when I say "no one," I only wish to designate those who believe that they give proof of intelligence by conforming themselves to the ways of today and even to the ways of the day after tomorrow.

As for me, I find only one commonplace word to explain my own position: I will say that the ways of today, the ways of so-called "meaning of history" have a taste of "ashes" to me. But, Lord, You well know that I firmly believe that You are the Strongest. Is it necessary to clarify this? Yes, in these present days. Yes, I believe it to be indispensable, because people now put their confidence in the power of man, a power that can launch rockets but allows people to die from hunger, a power that puts machines to work, but is also their oppressed slave . . .a power that pretends to have no use for God, but knows how to trick people in discussing the creation of the world.

I must stop talking. I must calm myself.

All that precedes so far is only destined, by modesty, to delay the moment when I must introduce myself to the reader.

Well, I am only a mere nurse, who has nevertheless seen many persons die and who continues to believe in the Mercy of God, and who has experienced how the Will of the Invisible God reveals itself at the right moment.

I am only a nurse, and I saw—in a country that I will not name, in a hospital that must remain anonymous—I saw a man die following an automobile accident, a man without a name, without a nationality, I mean, without identification papers.

Nevertheless, he had in his briefcase documents I was forced to examine. One of these documents began by these words: "I am the man without a name, the man without a family, without a country and without a heritage."

Apparently, this text of about one hundred type-written pages could bring no clue allowing one to identify this injured man. But who knows.

Moreover, let me be honest and, since I have spoken of confession, let me be completely honest about it: I already had decided to read these intimate notes. So I gave in quickly to this temptation. I could not foresee that, by letting my feminine curiosity stifle my scruples as a nurse. . .that I should come upon a veracious document that would upset and overwhelm me.

As this text was too serious to be simply thrown into the fire, too "compelling" to be entrusted into anybody's hands, [or it] seemed too truthful to me, especially to me, a former Protestant converted to the Holy Catholic and everlasting Church, to the Holy Church in which only it is required to try to practice a small or great but especially persevering holiness, that [as all this seemed to be true], I could not avoid giving precedence to the defense of my Holy Church above all other considerations. Oh, I know very well that God does not need to be defended, that He has no need of me, but I also know that He could in the past have left me in error, in the sadness of unanswered questions, in the atmosphere of a supreme presumption which, for example, has kept the Irish Catholics in ghettos for four centuries, where laws pretending to be legitimate and sacred acted as a barbed wire fence.

Not that I am Irish. Do not try to find out who I am; you will never do so. But the Irish, without being aware of it, have helped me to show some courage. At least may this humble testimony make up for what souls of great wisdom and of high standing forget to accomplish. But my injured patient was not Irish either. He seemed to be more or less a Slav. But this is not particularly important, since he could not speak.

Nevertheless, I tried to get some information from him by asking him to close his eyelids every time he wished to answer in the affirmative. At that time I had not yet read the document that he carried with him. But either he refused to answer my questions, or he did not have the strength to do so. How will I ever know?

It is only after his death that I realized, in reading the text, that he must have suffered a thousand times more in thinking of these hundred pages that he should never have had the weakness of writing than he suffered from his wounds and fractures.

If I had only known the immense power, the unbelievable importance of this man, reduced to the state of a broken puppet, I might have found the words that he needed to hear. I might have been able to destroy the armor that he had invented to shield his spite (why not simply say his suffering?). An armor, even strengthened by years of work, can also be destroyed in a fraction of a second. God and the Saints know this.

But I was only occupied with my work as a nurse; no this is not quite true; as for me (and that is not to be found in my books, my courses nor my examinations), prayer is complementary to medical care. And I prayed for this man who, I was told, possessed no identification papers.

I gave him a name. I called him Michael, because this Archangel often helped me. This Latin word Michael consoled me for having to listen in our new religious ceremonies—as noisy as our streets, our stadiums and our radios—to all those new words to which was added the adjective vernacular to impress and silence us. For, all this is comedy, all those speeches by which we are invited to participate as adults (while Christ called to Himself little children) is but derision trying to disguise some kind of ironical and cruel authoritativeness, but [which is] apt to turn against itself.

Therefore, I prayed for that man, naming him Michael and without suspecting that he was one of our worst enemies. Had I known it, my Christian duty would always have been to pray for him, to urge others to pray for him with unequaled ardor.

Now I have had Masses offered for him, but it is difficult to find Masses that keep the absolute appearance of a thousandfold holy Sacrifice and that have not the pitiful aspect of a pleasant meal. Alas, thrice alas!

Michael had an unforgettable look in his eyes, but one which I could not read.

After having received knowledge of his confidences, I tried to revive in myself the power of that look in order to discover in it what he wished me to do with his memoirs.

But, first of all, why had he written them?

Was there not in this a sign of real weakness, maybe the only dangerous weakness to which he had given in? What was his aim? Was it one of domination or of consolation? Only God knows.

Today I met a girlfriend who wishes that this text be published.

But have I a right to do this?

My greatest sorrow consists in confirming that I could never wish to ask that question in Confession, as I would have done some years ago.

No, the very holy virtue of obedience is today the extremely powerful weapon that our enemies, who pretend to be our friends, make use of against what we were, to put up in its stead, what they have decided to have us become.

In short, this word "become" can be described, because it is known; it already has four centuries of existence, and it is called Protestantism.

There it is: We are invited bit by bit, little obedience by little obedience, from false humility to false remorse, from deceitful charity to deceptive ambiguity, from words disguised as a double-edged word, of which "yes" is "no" and "no" is "yes"— we are invited, I say, to pretend to remain good Catholics all the while becoming perfect Protestants.

This is a brilliant idea, but, after all, someone had to think of it.

Yes, such is the Christianity today that some pretend to make us love.

But history teaches us who is the most Patient, who is the Strongest, who is the most Faithful.

May Michael forgive me if I reveal his role, for it is for his good and ours also.

*"Ad Majorem Dei Gloriam."* ["To the greater honor and glory of God."]

# Table of Contents

# 1

## *How The Man Without A Name Is Willing To Reveal The Greatest Mystery Of His Life*

I ask myself why I feel like writing my memoirs. It is rather strange. I believe that I write them because I do so every night in my dreams, whence a kind of complicity that forces me, I imagine, to continue during the daytime. But it matters not; no one will ever read them; I will destroy them in due time.

---

I am the man without a name, the man without a family, without a country and without heritage. I am one of those people whom bourgeois and bureaucrats despise. On account of this and of those who have wanted to be good to me, I have suffered stupidly. If only I had known what happiness would come from it! But I was too young to guess that from misfortune can spring up "rockets and suns."

1

I was at first the small boy without a name. I seemed to be three years old. I was crying and dragging myself on a Polish road. This was in 1920. Therefore, I can safely presume that I was born in 1917. But where and from whom? It seems that I could scarcely speak, that my Polish was very poor and my Russian still worse. I did not appear to understand German. Who was I? I could not even say my name any more. For, after all, I had had a name and I had answered to the call of my name. Hereafter, I will have to be content with the name chosen by my adoptive parents.

Even today, after fifty years, a wave of anger, although much lessened, crosses my heart every time that I recall Doctor and Mrs. X_____. They were good, they were generous, they were magnanimous. They had no child and they adopted me. They loved me more, I believe, than a child of their own. They loved me, because I had dragged them out of the despair in which sterility had plunged them.

I believe that they considered me as a gift from Heaven. For they had such a strong piety that they referred to God all that happened to them. Of course, they taught me, as if it were a game, to do likewise. Their virtue was so great that I never heard them speak ill about anyone.

At the time they found me, crying alone on a road, they were still young, about 35 years of age.

They were very good-looking and I was quickly sensitive to the almost exaggerated love that united them. When they looked at each other, then kissed, a pleasant feeling plunged me into delight. They were *my* father and *my* mother and I would say these possessive adjectives with a very juvenile ardor. My mother, especially, showed me such excessive love that I should have become unbearable. I do not know why it was not so. I was naturally calm and studious. I gave them no trouble. Not that I was girlish. I could fight quite well. To fight, it is not necessary to be violent or to be endowed with a bad character. My parents, especially my mother, thought that I had a good character, but they did not notice that, by a happy coincidence, my will agreed with theirs. I was very ambitious, and they approved of it. A boy does not ask for anything more.

In the year that I became fourteen years old, since I had achieved much success in my studies, it was decided that we would visit Rome and Paris. I was so happy that I tried to sleep less and less. Sleep seemed lost time to me, and I wanted to prepare for this trip. I read up on these two cities in advance, so to say.

One night, when my eyelids refused to obey me and to stay open, I imagined that my father must have some kind of medicine to keep sleep away. So I tiptoed to the parlor. They were in the adjoining room and were talking about me. They were worried about my passport, saying that *I was not their son.*

It was like a thunderbolt, do you know? At least that is what novelists say in like circumstances. But, I say that it is still worse and that human language simply has no word to express such abomination. And the pain that begins at that moment has the particularity of being immeasurable and as small as a newborn baby. Like a baby, it will grow and become stronger, but its victim is unaware of it.

I would have wished to die, and my heart seemed to go that way. How fast my heart beat while all the rest of myself seemed to be transformed into granite! When my heart came back to its normal pulse, I could again move. My body ached from head to toe. I did not know pain; that is why its first visit seized me completely and it took command of my life for a certain time. My pain urged me to leave, and I did so at once, without bringing anything with me. I would even have liked to leave naked, so as to owe nothing to those people.

For surely they were and are always "those people." The hatred that I feel for them matches the love that they showed me. For they always lied to me, even if they really loved me. That I will never forgive them for; I forgive nothing, by principle. If I were logical, I would be grateful to them. It is thanks to them if I am today one of the most redoubtable secret agents. I have become God's personal enemy, the one who has decided to have taught and proclaimed in the whole world the death of a God who in fact has never existed.

My pain urged me to run as far as Vladivostock. And I started out. But after a few thousand minutes, although I was a husky boy, I had to lean against a wall to regain my breath. The wall became a cloud to me, and I slid to the ground, stunned; at the same time, a far-off voice was saying, "Oh, he is a poor boy!"

I turned around with the intention of strangling the woman trying to show me some kind of maternalism.

My homicidal project was checked by disgust. I would never touch, even with the tips of my fingers, the skin of such a hideous person. I tried to speak, but I choked. Two women were trying to make me drink alcohol. I spat it out and immediately fell asleep. Broad daylight woke me up. A woman sitting at the foot of my bed was looking at me. Thence she had carried me. She might have been the same woman, but she no longer had make-up on her face. I said to her: "You are less disgusting than you were last night." She answered calmly, "Than the day before yesterday." That was why I was so hungry. I asked for something to eat, because women are destined to feed men. Might as well let her know at once that I would ask nothing else of her. I must say that she brought me heaps of good things.

I was beginning to soften when she said to me, "You have run away from home. You are 'so and so.'" I answered nothing, waiting for what was to come next. She added, "I can help you to cross into Russia." "How do you know that I wish to go to Russia?" "You spoke in your sleep." "So that is how you have learned my name?" "No. It was in the newspaper. Your parents beg you to return. They promise not to scold you." "I have no parents."

She must have understood that I had decided not to return because she said, "I have relatives in Russia. I can help you, help you to cross the border."

It was like a flash of light for me. So I asked her if she would agree to carry a letter to a comrade of mine, who would return from class at noontime. She seemed pleased to be able to do something for me. I prepared a short note in code. Happily, we had this habit to amuse ourselves and no one ever knew anything about it. In this dramatic circumstance, I could therefore make use of what had seemed to be just play for us. The pal in question was rich, and his parents were spoiling him outrageously by giving him much more money than he needed. I hoped that on this day he had some substantial savings destined to buy something completely useless. I knew that the friendship he felt for me—I mean that we felt for one another—would pass before anything else and that he would send me all the money that he could spare, all the more so because I did not hide from him my intention of crossing secretly into Russia, a country that he admired for its audacity. In fact, as he did not get along well with his father, he preferred Russia, his mother's country; and I knew that, although he envied me, he would have died rather than admit that he had some information about my running away. I even remembered that an uncle of his was a civil servant, at Leningrad, I believe. I asked him the address of this uncle and a word of recommendation. At the moment the woman was about to leave, I quickly added a post-scriptum, saying, "I want to enter the Party and to become someone great in the Party." It was to be my vengeance. The woman waited in front of my friend's door until he would return from school. She was lucky, because that day he returned at two p.m.

My friend recognized her and gave her a parcel. It contained a long coded letter for me, a letter in regular wording for the uncle, and a nice bundle of money. A real good guy!

I will not divulge, for reasons easily guessed, how I came to pass the border and to end up at Leningrad.

But, on the other hand, my first visit to the Uncle had something of an unforgettable character, since I know it by heart and I amuse myself at reliving it periodically.

I ignored what position the Uncle occupied

in the Russian administration, but I decided to be frank with him.

If I wanted to reach the rank that I had set for myself, I thought it better to play the game of frankness with this unique man.

I think that he understood me very well at this very first visit and that I pleased him.

The Uncle told me that I would have to study first of all the doctrine of the Party and languages.

All would depend on the quality of my studies. I answered that in everything I would always be first, and that I would soon know more than my professors.

It is agreeable to have someone with whom you can show your true self. He was the only one. I told him so. He was flattered, although he answered me with a slightly ironical smile.

At that moment, I undoubtedly was stronger than he, and I felt a wave of joy invading me, the first since I had run away. It did not last long, but it seemed to me a good omen, just the same.

I studied ferociously for six years. My two only joys were my trimestrial visit to the Uncle and my hatred for God, with the certainty of becoming the unquestioned Chief of Universal Atheism.

# 2

## *How We Discover That Misfortune Works To Fortify Human Beings*

The Uncle was my sole friend, the only man who truly knew me. For all others, I wished to be insignificant and I easily succeeded.

Women did not interest me; I even had a certain aversion for them and, as a consequence, for the idiots who love them too much. My determination to learn the maximum was greatly helped by an astonishing memory. After reading a book attentively, I knew it by heart, even if it were written in a pretentious style. But I also had the faculty of retaining only what was worthwhile. My distinctly superior intelligence would retain only the valuable ideas, and I knew how to criticize even the greatest professors. My liking for atheistic doctrines, which are the basis and foundation of the Party, exalted my zeal, which was unbounded.

At the end of six years of arduous studies, the

Uncle summoned me one evening to his office. Until then, he had received me at his home.

On that day, I noticed that he was really a high police officer, as I had always supposed him to be.

He made me a tough proposal, capable, he thought, of upsetting me. He said to me: "I am now going to send you to practice a militant and international atheism. You will have to fight all religions, but principally the Catholic, which is better organized. To do so, you will enter a seminary and become a Roman Catholic priest."

A moment of silence—during which I let joy pervade me while I kept an appearance of total indifference—was my only answer. The Uncle was satisfied and he did not hide it. With the same calm, he continued: "To be able to enter a seminary, you will have to return to Poland, reconcile yourself with your adoptive family, and present yourself to the bishop." I had a short feeling of revolt. Since the beginning of my connections with the Uncle, it was the first time that I did not master myself. He seemed to be satisfied and amused by it. "So," he said, "you are not totally made of marble." This reflection made me furious, and I answered dryly, "I am and I shall remain so whatever happens."

The Uncle seemed to be relaxed and even amused, as if my career, my vocation, my future (and therefore that of the Party) did not depend upon the decisions taken on this day.

He added: "Marble is a beautiful thing, of primordial use for one who wishes to become a secret agent, but on this occasion it is necessary that you show to your family the greatest affection." I felt like a coward and asked in a pitiful tone, "During six years of seminary?" He answered me with the harshness shown toward the guilty: "And if I said yes, what would you answer?" It was easy for me to reply that I would submit, and I was surprised to feel more witty than he. He kept on smiling and said to me: "Yes, you were not able to hide that you thought me to be an idiot who was naively showing his hand." I turned red, something that never happens to me. He added: "A secret agent has no blood in his veins, no heart, loves no one, not even himself. He is the thing of the Party, which will devour him alive and without warning. Keep this well in mind, that wherever you will be, we will watch you and get rid of you at your first imprudence. It is to be well understood that if you are in danger, even without its being your fault, you must not rely upon us. You will be disavowed." I answered: "I know all that, but I never hid from you the hatred that I feel for them." "Hatred, except the hatred of God, at Lenin's example, does not enter into our services," he replied. "I need you to be accepted by a true bishop of your native country, Poland. But, we do not intend to have you pursue your religious studies in that country. No, you will be sent to a country across the Atlantic, but this is confidential, and you will simulate surprise when you receive that order. Yes, we are led to fear a European war with that fool who rules Germany. Therefore, it seems wiser to have you study somewhere else, Canada, for example. We have another motive also; it is that European Seminaries are much more strict than those of America."

I made an imperceptible gesture of protest, which was immediately detected. The Uncle kept on saying: "I know that you could endure six years of very strict seminary life without ever going out, but that is not the point. We need to have you learn what is going on in the world, and it is wise to be able to speak to the world in order to make it lose its faith, and it is to be understood, without ever being suspected. It would be of no avail to send young men to seminaries if they got caught. No, you will remain a priest until death, and you will behave as a faithful and chaste priest. Anyway, I know you, you are an intellectual." Then, he gave me a few precisions on the operation of the service into which I was going to enter and at the head of which I hoped to end my days.

As soon as I entered the seminary, I was supposed to try to discover how to destroy all that was taught to me. But, to do so, I should have to study attentively and intelligently—that is, without passion—the history of the Church. I would particularly never lose sight of the fact that persecutions

only make martyrs of whom Catholics have had reason to say that they are the seed of Christians. Therefore, no martyrs. I must never forget that all religions
are based on fear, the ancestral fear; all religions
are born from this fear. Therefore, if you suppress
fear, you suppress religions. But that is not sufficient. "It is up to you," he told me, "to discover
the right methods." I was swimming in joy. He
added: "You will write to me every week, very
shortly, to mention all the slogans that you wish
to spread in the world, with a brief explanation of
the reasons that have prompted you to choose them.
At the end of a certain time, more or less long,
you will be put into direct action with the network.
That is, you will have ten persons under your orders,
and each of these ten will also have ten other persons under their orders.

"The ten persons who will be directly under
your orders will never know you. To reach you, they
will have to pass through me. Thus you will never
be denounced. We already have in our service
numerous priests in all countries where Catholicism is implanted, but you will never know one
another. One is a bishop. Maybe you will enter into
contact with him; it will depend upon the rank that
you reach. We have spies everywhere and particularly old ones, who follow the press of the whole
world. A resumé will be sent to you regularly. We
will easily know when your own ideas have made
their way into peoples' minds. See, an idea is good
when some idiot writer presents it as one of his

own. Nobody is more conceited than a writer. We rely much on such writers and we do not have to train them. They work for us without knowing it, or rather without wanting to."

I asked him how I could reach him if war broke out. He had foreseen everything. I would receive, in due time, a letter mailed from a free country and out of reach of hostilities.

I would recognize such a letter to be valid because it would contain my secret appellation, that is "AA-1025." "AA" meant "Anti-Apostle." I was therefore led to think that the number 1025 was my service number. To my great surprise, I had guessed right. Therefore I cried out, "1,024 priests or seminarians have entered this career before me." "That is correct," he answered coldly. I was not discouraged, but hurt and furious. I would have willingly strangled those 1,024 men. I only said, "Do you really need that many?" The Uncle only smiled. It was useless to hope that I could conceal my thoughts. So I added pitifully, "One must believe that they did not accomplish much good work, if you continue to recruit more of them."

But he would not satisfy my curiosity. I wished at least to learn if I could come into contact with some of them. But the Uncle assured me that I would never know even one of them. I did not understand. I felt disconcerted. "How," I told him, "can we accomplish good work if we are dispersed and deprived of coordination and competition?" "As for coordination," he replied, "do not worry, we have seen to that, but only those who hold rank know how it functions. As for competition, we rely on the love of the Party."

I had nothing more to answer. Could I say that the Party would not realize anything worthwhile in atheism until I became head of that service? I was so firmly convinced that it was so that I relegated my 1,024 predecessors to the category of absent ticket-holders.

# 3

## *How Pride Is Exalted As A Dominant And Superb Quality*

After this memorable evening, the Uncle invited me to learn of some secret and really thrilling papers. Although these memoirs will never be published, I wish to remain prudent, so I will not speak of these papers. I know some people who would give a fortune, even today, to be able to photograph them. It makes me laugh, because it would only suffice to invent a machine that could read my memory. During that same week, I learned a certain number of useful addresses and telephone numbers in different countries.

All these precautions meant that war was close at hand. I felt an impatient desire to leave Europe, because the welfare of humanity would have been endangered by my death or even only by the degradation brought about by an extended military service.

The Uncle made me return to his office to discuss international politics, but I was not deeply interested in that science. The Uncle blamed me for this, specifying that atheism was only a branch of politics. In my inner self, I thought that atheism was the most important. And the Uncle, who seemed to hear my thoughts, added, "You are right to consider atheism as primordial, as fundamental, but you still have much to learn in this matter." I agreed with the most perfect bad faith. And while keeping my impassivity, I added, "Nevertheless, I have a special idea on the general direction to be given to the fight that we are to undertake."

A flash of amusement passed on the Uncle's face. I believe that it was because he really loved me. I stared at him with a bit of defiance. He said to me, "Speak, but be brief." What more did I want? I therefore said very quietly, "Instead of fighting religious sentiment, we ought to prompt it in a utopian direction." He kept silent; he was digesting my idea. "Good," he said, "give me an example."

I held the long end of the stick.

In fact, it seemed to me that the whole world was in my hands at that moment. I calmly explained: "You must drive into the head of men, and particularly into the head of Churchmen, to search for, at any price, a universal religion into which all churches would be melded together. So that this idea could take form and life, we must inculcate in pious people, especially Roman Catholics, a feeling of guilt concerning the unique truth in which they pretend to live." "Are you not yourself utopian in the second part of your proposition?" "No, no, not at all," I replied vividly. I was Catholic, and very Catholic, I mean, very pious and zealous until my fourteenth year, and I believe it to be rather easy to show Catholics that there are other holy persons among the Protestants, the Moslems and the Jews, etc., etc.... "Let us admit this," he answered me, "but then what sentiment will the other religions have?" "It will vary," said I, "and I still must study this aspect of the problem; but for me, it is essential to strike deeply and definitely at the Catholic Church. It is the most dangerous one." "And how would you see this Universal Church to which you would like to have all churches run?" "I see it very simple," said I, "it could not be otherwise but simple. So that all men could enter it, it could retain a vague idea of a God, more or less Creator, more or less Good, according to the times. Moreover, this God will be useful only in periods of calamity. Then the ancestral fear will fill these temples, but in other times, they will be rather empty." The Uncle thought it over a good while, then he said to me, "I fear that the Catholic clergy will quickly notice the danger and be hostile to your plan." I replied sharply, "This is what has happened until now. My idea was launched by non-Catholics, and the Catholic Church has always closed its door to such a program. It is precisely why I wanted to study the way to make it change its mind. I know that this will not be easy, that we will have to work hard at it, during twenty or even fifty years, but how we should succeed in the end." "By what means?" "By numerous and subtle means. I look at the Catholic Church as if it were a sphere. To destroy it, you must attack it in numerous small points until it loses all resemblance to what it was before. We will have to be very patient. I have many ideas that might seem at first sight to be petty and childish, but I maintain that the entirety of those petty childishnesses will become an invisible weapon of great efficacy." "Well," the Uncle told me, "you will have to prepare me a short plan of your project." Slowly, I picked up my portfolio, took out an envelope which contained the precious work of the development of my ideas. I laid this document on his desk with invisible satisfaction. The Uncle started at once to read it, something I never dared to hope. This proved to me that he was laying great hopes in me. How he had reason to do so, the dear old man!

After his reading it, which took him more time than necessary, the Uncle looked at me and said: "I will have this work examined by my counselors. You will return for an answer in eight days, at this same hour. Meanwhile, prepare your departure for Poland. Take this," he told me, extending to me an envelope that was generously filled with roubles, more than I had ever possessed.

I took in plenty of theaters and movies and

bought a large number of books. I did not know how to ship them, but I thought that the Uncle could see to that by some kind of diplomatic shipping container.

I lived these eight days in such a state of exaltation that I could no more feel my body and could scarcely sleep.

To me the question came up (and it was the first time) to decide whether I should try to meet a woman. But in the state of mental excitement that I found myself in, I thought that it was not worthwhile. I even feared that such a lowly animal action might bring bad luck to my project, actually being studied by the highest authorities of the service. Was it not important, before all else, that I should, then and there, jump over many ranks and go ahead of the largest number possible of the 1,024 predecessors of mine, who could not surely be so worthy as I was?

One night, I tried to intoxicate myself to find out if my brains would receive a useful impulse from it. But nothing came out of it, and I can affirm that alcohol is more harmful than religion—and that is saying a lot.

When the time came to present myself again at the Uncle's office, my heart was beating a little more quickly than normal, but it was not disagreeable. The important thing was that no one would notice it.

The Uncle looked at me a long time, then told me with a half-smile that his chief wanted to become acquainted with me.

As it was certain that such a high official would not put himself out just to let me know his displeasure, I was not at all impressed by this convocation. But, on the other hand, I was horrified by the exterior aspect of this famous "chief."

Horrified is the correct word to use and, thirty years later, I only have to close my eyes to see him again and to feel his presence.

He has such a "presence" that all the others seemed to be only puppets.

I still hate that feeling, but I must add that this "presence" of his was that of a monster. How can one accumulate, in one and the same person, brutality, coarseness, ruse, sadism, vulgarity? This man must surely be one of those who visit prisons in order to delight themselves in tortures. But, I have a deep disgust for cruelty, which is, I am sure, a sign of weakness. And as I despise all kinds of weaknesses, how could I ever accept the Uncle's showing himself so servile in the presence of the brute who received us. The brute acted like all chiefs; he began by looking fixedly into my eyes to see. To see what? With me, there is nothing to see. "There will never be anything to see, Comrade," thought I with satisfaction.

Then the Chief asked me what I cared for the most. It was easy for me to say: "The triumph of the Party," whereas the truth held more subtlety. Did the chief have none? It was unthinkable. Then he added in a slightly neglected tone: "From now on, you are on the list of our active secret agents. You will give orders every week. I rely on your zeal. I readily admit that it will take a long time to destroy all religions from within; nevertheless, it is necessary that the orders which you will give find an echo, notably among writers, journalists and even theologians. It is to be understood that we have a team who watches the religious writings of the whole world and gives its advice on the usefulness of directives given by such or such an agent. Therefore, do your best to please. I have high hopes, because it seems to me that you have already understood it all by yourself."

The brute was not an idiot. He would hear about my work; of this I was sure.

I know too well the vulnerability of Christians to doubt of my future success. I believe that this vulnerability can be entitled "Charity."

At the mention of this sacro-sanct word charity, we can inoculate them with any kind of remorse. And remorse is always a state of lowered resistance.

It is at the same time medical and mathematical, which, even though they do not go together, nevertheless I marry those two elements.

I saluted the Chief in a dignified manner and thanked him coldly. I did not wish him to imagine that he had impressed me.

I was again alone with the Uncle.

I refrained from making the least comment on this so very famous chief.

Rather, I congratulated myself that this personage was so unpleasant, because I was cured in advance of all timidity toward the great of this world. And I always came to the same conclusion, that all in all, I was the greatest!

# 4

## *How The Art Of Playing The Comedy Of Modesty Meets With A Perfectly Humble Obstacle*

I left for Poland, trying to convince myself that my power of dissimulation meant that I had certain gifts as an actor.

At twenty-one years old, after six years of solitude as a poor and ambitious student, I had to become again a loving, obliging, obedient and pious young man—more than pious, simply dying to enter a seminary. A nice act for my debut.

I thought that I could easily deceive my so-called mother, but what about the doctor? I really feared his diagnosis. That man was probably the only one whom I feared in my life. Nevertheless, I must at all cost, at any price whatsoever, fool him too. Not that I could not enter a seminary without his help, but to prove my strength, I must never be suspected.

The doctor was for me a test of my own worth.

I rang the "home" bell at about six o'clock p.m., so as to be a short hour with her, before his return.

It was she who opened the door to me.

She had aged very much and had no make-up on her face. She seemed ill. She began to tremble, then started to cry. Women are really where they belong when they are in harems, where men visit them only in case of absolute necessity.

I asked her forgiveness for my long silence, hoping that this question of repentance would be quickly settled and forgotten before the doctor came in.

I had no idea of manifesting male repentance in the presence of a true male. With her, I knew that we would quickly come to the joy of meeting again and to plans for the future. As she could not have a greater desire than of wanting me to become a Catholic priest, I told her at once of my compelling vocation.

The poor, stupid woman was so happy that I could have made her believe anything. She wanted to know how the idea of this beloved vocation had come to me.

I had vaguely thought of various explanations, but I rejected preparing such a scene in advance.

Generally, what is premeditated does not sound so well as what is invented on the spot. I made up a story of an apparition quite proper to win her. I knew that the doctor was suspicious of such things. But she had a weakness for the mysterious. Thus, I was sure to divide them and strengthen my position. While they discussed me, they would leave me alone.

I therefore told her a story of a heavenly apparition, being careful to stamp in my memory all its details, so as never to contradict myself.

I thought that it was ironic to pretend that I had had a visit from St. Anthony of Padua. Could not the Patron Saint of Lost Objects also look after lost children?

This Saint is so popular that you can impute to him any miracle whatsoever; pious people will always fall for it. Therefore, St. Anthony of Padua visited me, evidently, with the little Child Jesus in his arms.

While I was at it, I might as well make of it a beautiful devotional picture. As we were "floating" in the most syrupy piety, the Doctor entered. I was relieved to see a reasonable being come in. But I saw at once that he did not believe me. Thus, the game would be a hard one to win, but therefore more amusing. It was up to me to convince my foster father. I had to bring him at least to pretend that he believed me. But this first evening was rather distressing. The doctor is one of the rare men, really intelligent, whom I have met. The "game" was all the more pleasing.

The following day, I asked them to meet the bishop. My foster mother knew him since childhood. He received me nicely, but without enthusiasm. He must be one of those Catholics who think that it is better not to excite a vocation, but on the contrary, to oppose it. A real vocation must triumph over all obstacles.

Happily, I knew well this state of mind, and I was not vexed by it. But I acknowledge that such an attitude can cause confusion in someone who has no vocation. As for me, I knew how to remain Christianly humble, and it seemed impossible that the bishop should be displeased with me.

Nevertheless, he requested that I present myself to the pastor of my parish and also to a religious noted for having the gift of mind-reading. This gibberish simply meant that this good man was capable of detecting false vocations from the simply imaginary to the frankly perverse.

I first went to see my pastor, a brave and very simple man. He was hoping to see a vocation blossom in his parish, and he would have given me all that he possessed, that is, almost anything to announce this happy news.

In order that my holy enthusiasm would be of some benefit to me in the doctor's mind, I asked my foster mother to invite this clergyman to dinner. It was delightful, because this man had the soul of a child and, in the presence of this rare phenomenon, but deeply appreciated in a trial of canonization, the doctor felt ill. How can an honest Christian resist Saints?

I was therefore much comforted when I went to meet the religious whose perspicacity was so highly praised.

At first sight, this man seemed to me hard to bear, on account of his slowness and the frequent silences that he seemed to affect.

Nevertheless, I could bring out all the cliches apt to describe a true priestly vocation. I laughed in my inner self, because, of course, how could this man imagine that my secret thoughts could be revealed to him? And how could he know that I had secret thoughts? Our interview was lengthy, but I at last took a liking to it. I spoke with facility and listened to myself with satisfaction.

Of course, I manifested the most exquisite modesty. It is indeed a self-styled virtue very easy to imitate. It is even a very amusing game. And I was an ace at modesty, as well as of many other acts.

I dared not speak of my supposed apparition

of St. Anthony of Padua. Thus, in case my mother had revealed this fact to him, he would be edified to see that I kept silence about it.

Nevertheless, I was proud to let him know that I never had any connection with a woman and that I was altogether disinterested in that sex, only good for procreation.

I thought that this ought to be a certain sign of a vocation.

I thought that I could use the word vocation to express the trade that I had chosen in the ranks of the Party and that my indifference toward women became a kind of predestination. An Apostle, or Anti-Apostle, must marry only his Apostolate.

I was therefore very eloquent each time that the word apostolate would return to our conversation.

It must have seemed evident that I would become a very zealous priest. This religious tried to lay me many traps, notably to bring me to lie. Childish business! An intelligent man knows that lying must not be used, or very rarely. And even when I felt obliged to tell lies, I have too much memory to contradict myself by revealing the truth. No, a good lie must simply become a truth for him who creates it, and also for all his listeners.

This religious wanted to know why I had left my adoptive parents for six years without news.

Then, I became moved. It was easy to review the past and live again the vague pain that had prompted me to leave for Russia. But, justifiably, this prudent man seemed to fear that I had become a Communist. I told him that I was not interested in politics. As for my six years of silence, I was simply not able to explain them.

I believe it to be a good thing to appear sometimes as a feeble and vulnerable man. The people in command are then very happy to protect you.

I even insisted, saying that this silence would be the remorse of my whole life, letting him understand that my mother felt rewarded for it by my priestly vocation.

Thus, the old man would not want to hurt my mother's feelings by taking away from her the only joy of her old age. Obviously, I did not use such imprudent words, but only hoped inwardly that it would be so.

As our conversation went on, it became more and more cordial. I was very satisfied and we parted as friends.

Many days went by without news, as if the Church were not in a hurry to have one more seminarian.

On my part, I worked with ardor on the next directives which would reach the whole world, by way of Russia.

When at last I was called to the bishop's house, the earth seemed to open up in front of me, because the bishop quietly told me that the religious thought that I did not have a vocation.

# 5

## *How An Ambitious Anti-Christian Program Leads First To Assassination*

My mother fell sick and was put under observation at the hospital. My father, by a strange reaction of pity, I suppose, played the whole scale of kindness with me. I responded with great dignity. He asked me what I intended to do. I answered him that I would not quit, but that I would study medicine, if the Church really did not want me—it was a little exposé on the welfare of bodies which favors the good of the soul. But enough of self-praise.

Of course, I had sent an urgent telegram to the Uncle. Through the priest who acted as my mail box, the answer came rapidly. It was short and it only half surprised me. It read: "Suppress the obstacle."

Of course, I had received a special training reserved to secret agents.

I knew as well how to attack as how to defend myself. On this occasion, I debated a long time with myself in order to know whether I should simulate an accident or rather heart failure. In short, should I sow worry, or simply give proof of my docility.

I thought it best to perform this liquidation outside the convent. Consequently, I prayed my correspondent to invite this religious to his house, under any pretext. Happily, these two men knew each other.

I was not lying when I asserted that I wanted to know what had prompted this religious to refuse me the signs of a true vocation. This was important for me, because I could learn how to perfect my little religious act. Moreover, I was terribly vexed by this setback. And I still hoped to bring this religious to reverse his decision.

While waiting for this second interview, I worked carefully at my real task.

I wrote the following: "It is very important that Christians become conscious of the scandal that is caused by the division of the Church. For, there are three kinds of Christianity: the Catholic, a number of Orthodox and some three hundred Protestant sects."

To emphasize the last prayer of Jesus of Nazareth, a prayer that was never heard: "Be ONE, as my Father and I are ONE." To cultivate a growing remorse in this regard, particularly among Catholics.

To stress that Catholics are responsible for the division among Christians, because, by their refusal to compromise, they caused schisms and heresies. To come to a point that every Catholic will feel so guilty that he will wish to atone at any price. To suggest to him that he must himself endeavor to find all the means capable of bringing Catholics closer to Protestants (and also to others) without harming the Credo. To keep only the Credo. And again . . . attention: The Credo must undergo a very slight modification. The Catholics say, "I believe in the Catholic Church." The Protestants say, "I believe in the Universal Church." It is the same thing. The word Catholic means "universal."

At least, it was so at the origin of the Church. But in the course of ages, the word "Catholic" took a deeper meaning. It has become almost a magic word. And I say that we must suppress it from the Credo, for the best interests of all, that is, the union with Protestants.

Moreover, it will be necessary that each Catholic endeavor to find out what would please Protestants, since faith and the Credo are not at stake, and never will be.

Always drive minds toward a greater charity,

a larger fraternity. Never talk about God, but about the greatness of man. Bit by bit, transform the language and the attitude of mind. Man must occupy the first place. Cultivate confidence in man, who will prove his own greatness by founding the Universal Church in which all good wills shall melt together. To bring it out that the good will of man, his sincerity, his dignity, are worth more than an always invisible God. To show that the luxury and art found in Catholic and Orthodox Churches are intensely disliked by Protestants, Jews and Moslems. To suggest that this useless show must be suppressed for a greater welfare. To excite an iconoclastic zeal. Youngsters must destroy all this hodgepodge: statues, pictures, reliquaries, priestly ornaments, organs, candles and votive lamps, stained glass, and cathedrals, etc., etc. . .

It would do some good that a prophecy be sent throughout the world that would be the following: "Someday, you will see married priests and Mass said in vernacular tongues." I remember with joy that I was the first one to say these things in 1938. That same year, I urged women to ask for the priesthood. And I advocated a Mass, not a parish Mass, but a family Mass that would be said at home, by the father and mother, before each meal.

Ideas crowded into my head, each one more exciting than the one before it.

As I was finishing transcribing into code this

entire program, my friend informed me that the religious was to visit him the next day.

I had decided my line of conduct, and I thought of trying to bring this quite simple and not very cultivated man to change his verdict.

He did not seem surprised to see me arrive. My friend had tried to make him talk about me, but to no avail, so he gave the conventional sign agreed upon.

I was not discouraged, but I attacked with mildness this certainly honest man. I pointed out to him that he was almost committing a murder by refusing me the priesthood. And I insisted on knowing the motives of his attitude. But he answered me that he had no motives, that the Lord enlightened him on souls and that mine was not worthy to enter the priesthood. I acknowledge that I became nervous. This was not an answer. But I finally believed that he did not lie.

In truth, he had no precise motive to reject me totally, except a sort of intuition, all that is of very little scientific nature. The worst was that he did not seem at all conscious of the unwarranted nature of his actions. He seemed to operate completely by magic.

I informed him that I had decided to present myself somewhere else. He answered me, with an angelical smile, that I was wrong in persisting.

I told him that I could even take away his life, if I could by that gesture succeed in entering the seminary. He answered that he knew it. Then and there, I was truly stupefied. And we remained silent a long while, looking at each other. And again he spoke, saying, "You do not know what you are doing." I admit that, at that moment, I would have liked to run away to the end of the world. That man possesed a power that I could not explain to myself.

But my friend made me a sign. He felt that I was weakening. And I knew that it would be the end for me if I disobeyed the orders of the Uncle.

I must myself make this obstacle disappear. My worth, although visible, must be confirmed by this gesture of obedience and courage.

Then I got up and caused death without wounds. Men of my worth have all the chance of undergoing a special training, whose precious secrets come from Japan.

At that time, few persons in the Occident were aware of being very ignorant of all the extraordinary possibilities which the human body offers for defense as well as for attack, even for murder, with bare hands. Although a Russian, I readily admit that in this matter (and maybe in others) the Japanese are experts. I do not believe that, at the time of my studies, many European, or even American countries taught really esthetic and at the same time efficacious methods of fighting with or without death, but always with the bare hands.

I was proud to be one of the first devotées of these martial arts, all the more so because they correspond—for the Russian that I am—to a national worship of the dance. They have allowed me, on many occasions, to defend myself without acting like a sluggish and prehistoric animal.

Having caused, in two swift gestures (but requiring a long training) the death without wound of the one who had the almost comical audacity to oppose himself to Marxism-Leninism (in other words, to the future), I quietly returned home. The death would naturally be published. Cause: heart failure.

The next day, my body was covered with pimples, I was furious, because it was a sign of weakness, a sign that my liver could not support such tension. I was stupid. But I congratulated myself because my father thought that I was really suffering on account of not entering the seminary, and he took pains to go plead my cause with the bishop—with success!

# 6

## How The Anti-Apostle Effectively Begins His Work And Feels A Very Special Hatred For The Cassock

I therefore prepared myself openly to enter the seminary.

And my mother, who was cured, made some ill-considered purchases for me, when the bomb exploded in the form of a telegram calling me to Rome and mentioning, "For a new assignment." I made believe that I did not understand. My mother again started to cry, and I heaved a sigh of relief when I left the country of my childhood days. I hoped never to return.

In Rome, I had very interesting conversations with a professor who would be mine when I would have received the priesthood. He was a member of our network. He was very optimistic. He had specialized in Holy Scripture and was working at a new translation of the Bible in English. The most astounding thing was that he had chosen a Lutheran pastor as his only collaborator. The said pastor, besides, was no longer in agreement with his own church, which seemed old-fashioned to him.

This collaboration, of course, remained secret. The aim of these two men was to rid humanity of all the systems which it had given itself through the Bible, and especially the New Testament. Thus, the virginity of Mary, the Real Presence of Christ in the Eucharist and His Resurrection, according to them, were to be set aside, in order to end up with a complete suppression. The dignity of modern man, in their eyes, was worth such a price.

The professor also taught me a reasonable way to say Mass, since in six years I would be obliged to say it.

While waiting for a profound modification of the whole ceremony, he never pronounced the words of the Consecration. But so as not to be suspected, he pronounced words almost similar, at least according to the ending of the words. He advised me to do the same. All that made this ceremony look like a sacrifice should, little by little, be suppressed. The whole ceremony should represent only a common meal, as among Protestants.

He even assured me that it should never have been otherwise. He also worked at the elaboration of a new Ordinary of the Mass and advised me also to do the same, because it appeared to him to be

altogether desirable to present to people a large
number of diversified Masses. There must be some,
very short, for families and small groups, some longer
ones, for Feast Days, although, according to him,
the real feast for the working classes is a walk in
Nature. He thought that we could easily arrive at
a point of considering Sunday as a day consecrated
to Nature.

He told me that his work did not leave him
enough time to ponder over Jewish, Moslem, Oriental and other religions, but that such a work was
of great importance, maybe more important than
his new translation of the Bible. He advised me
to search vigorously in all non-Christian religions
for what exalted man the most and to promote it.

I tried to bring him to talk about the other
priests and seminarians who were affiliated with
the Party like myself, but he pretended to know
practically nothing about them.

Nevertheless, he gave me the address of a
Frenchman, a professor of singing, who resided in
the city where I would go for six years to study
profoundly tedious subjects. He assured me that
I could have full confidence in this man, that he
would render me the most thoughtful services, as
for example, allowing me to keep my lay clothes
in his house, under condition that I pay him well.

Of course, he also made me go around Rome

and taught me all kinds of legends on the Saints who are the most revered in this city. There was enough reason to have them all erased from the calendar, which was also one of our objectives. But both of us knew that it would take more time to kill all the Saints than it would to kill God.

One day, while we were resting on the terrace of a cafe, he said to me: "Imagine this city without a single cassock, without a single religious costume, masculine or feminine. What emptiness! What marvelous emptiness! It is in Rome that I grasp the enormous importance of the cassock. And I swore to myself that it would disappear from our streets and even our churches, because one can easily say Mass in just his coat."

This little game, which consists in imagining our streets without cassocks, became a kind of reflex action for me. I gained from it an ever-growing hatred for this piece of black rag.

It seemed to me that the cassock spoke a mute but oh so eloquent language! All the cassocks were saying, to believers as well as to indifferent people, that the man thus veiled had given himself to an invisible God whom he pretended was all-powerful.

When I was myself obliged to put on this ridiculous robe, I promised myself two things: first, to understand why and how priestly vocations came to young boys, and secondly, to inculcate in all those who wore it the pious desire to take it off, in order better to influence the indifferent and our enemies.

I had promised myself to give this purpose all the appearances of great zeal. For me this is relatively easy. I had more difficulty in understanding the birth of a vocation in young boys. This birth was so simple that I could hardly believe it to be true. But, it does seem true that when young boys, between 4 and 10 years old, know a sympathetic priest, they have a desire to imitate him. And then and there I understood my hatred for the cassock— because those young boys would not have felt the real or imaginary power of the priest if he did not signalize himself by a life different from that of others.

The costume was one of these differences, and we can even say that the costume forever proclaimed all the doctrine of the man who wore it.

The cassock was for me like a marriage between God, described as all-powerful, and these men, manifesting at their every step their gift and separation.

The more I considered these things, the more I became angry. But I was also very grateful to life for having me live my childhood and even my adolescence in a very Catholic family, because I do believe that the worth of my Anti-Apostolate came from that fact. I knew that, on account of past experiences. I would be the best of agents, and consequently I was destined to become the grand chief of this profitable work. And I felt entitled to rejoice in advance because young boys, when they would meet priests living like all other people, would no longer desire to imitate them. They would also have to look at "everybody" and that would lead pretty far. The choice of truly imitable men would then be so great!

Besides, these new priests belonging to a church widely opened to all would not resemble one another. They would not have the same teaching at all. As they could not get along together, at least on theological grounds, each one would only have a few followers. And since they would fear the colleague living in the neighboring ward. . .in short, they could only agree on philanthropic questions. And God would be dead, that's all. But, after all, this is not something difficult, and I ask myself why nobody has as yet thought out this method. It is true that some centuries are more favorable than others for the blooming of certain flowers.

The beginning of my seminary life was a most happy one. My condition of an only and very cherished child of a rich family, who preferred separation to war, made of me an interesting subject. Everyone wished to show sympathy to the courageous young Polish man. The glory of God was more worthy to me than that of my country, they would say. What holiness! With modesty, I let them speak.

I had promised myself to be the first in everything, and it was so; my knowledge of living languages was really prodigious. This is, after all, common to Orientals. I worked with stubbornness on Latin and Greek. I was also authorized to follow special lessons in singing with my French friend. This seminary was not strict at all. The formation of character was not stressed as much as in Europe. I was also outstanding in competitive sports, but did not show my special knowledge of hand-to-hand fighting, a knowledge that came directly from Japan.

In short, all was going so well that I felt lonesome and was looking for some feat that would bring sparkle into my life.

I found nothing better than to confess myself to one of my professors who seemed the most attracted to me personally.

# 7

## *How The Hero Tries To Test The Secret Of Confession*

Therefore I confessed myself to a noble old man, the one we called, with true fondness, "Blue Eyes." Even I would sometimes fall under the spell of his childlike look. That is why I chose him for this experiment.

As for myself, I wanted to find out how he would act to keep the secret of Confession and, at the same time, to make use of it to have me dismissed. I did not think that it could be dangerous for me, because I could always deny everything. Moreover, I was the first in all things and therefore I was in very good standing. I was visibly the most intelligent of the whole crowd.

So I begged "Blue Eyes" to hear my confession and I related everything to him, at least the essentials, that I was a Communist, attached to the secret service section of militant atheism, that I had murdered a Polish religious who pretended that I had no vocation to the priesthood.

Strangely enough, "Blue Eyes" believed me at once. I could have invented the whole story. He had the trite reaction of speaking to me about my eternal salvation.

I almost broke out into laughter. Did he imagine that I had the least atom of faith?

I was obliged to explain clearly to him that I neither believed in God nor in the devil. Such a confession was probably something new to him. I almost pitied him.

He therefore said to me: "What do you expect to gain by entering Holy Orders?"

It was in all frankness that I clarified my intentions: "To destroy the Church from within." "You are quite conceited," he answered me.

I was almost becoming angry, and I was glad to reveal that we were already more than one thousand seminarians and priests. He answered me: "I do not believe you." "As you like, but my number is 1025 and, even supposing that some are dead, I can still say that we number about one thousand."

There was a long silence and he asked me dryly: "What do you want of me?"

It was difficult for me to answer that I had only wanted to amuse myself at finding how he would act with the secret of Confession. So I only said: "I suppose that you will try to have me dismissed?" "Dismiss you! Are you not the most brilliant of our students and one of the most pious?" It was I who no longer knew what to answer. Nevertheless, I told him: "Does my confession not enlighten you as to my true character?" He said to me: "Confession was instituted by Our Lord Jesus Christ for the welfare of souls; your confession is therefore useless." "Not even to understand me better?" "Not even for that, because when you will have left this place, I will have completely forgotten." "Really?" "You know that very well, since you are studying with us." "I know it theoretically, but how could I know it practically?" "So," he answered me, "here is the real aim of this unbelievable confession?" "Maybe." "If you have another aim, you had better tell me." "No," I replied to him gently, "I just wanted to study you, that is all."

He seemed to ponder; then he said to me: "It is a useless undertaking; nothing will come of it." "Nothing at all . . . really?" "Nothing at all, you know it." And he went away, leaving me crestfallen.

The next day, a classmate who thought himself a friend of mine because he liked me, told me in low tones: " 'Blue Eyes' prayed all night in the chapel." I watched the old professor; he did not seem to be one who had had a sleepless night. But, while he was droning his course, I was meditating upon that night which maybe might have been an imitation of the Agony in the Garden of Olives.

"Blue Eyes" must have prayed that this chalice would pass away from him. But it was in no one's power to get rid of this confession.

It seemed to me almost impossible for him to forget it. In his prayer he must have asked that I repent or leave. Did he not try also to find out how he could provoke my departure? And each time that this idea came back to his mind, he must have cried interiorly: "But no, since I know nothing."

What could he say against me that did not pertain to this confession? Simply nothing; I would not have confessed myself if I had not been the picture of a perfect seminarian.

Did not the poor old man know that a Communist is ready to make all sacrifices? All those people believe that only Christians perform sacrifices.

During the following days I observed "Blue Eyes" attentively, and I always found him to be himself as usual. He was just as calm, as gentle, as "blue," I should say.

Actually, I had a liking for him, and I almost accused myself of it when I wrote to the Uncle.

But I decided not to relate anything about this confession story; over there, they might not have understood.

Many months afterwards, I was seized again with the desire of confessing myself to other professors. Actually, I was keenly annoyed by the monotony of my life and by the fact that I seemed to please everybody. A little fight would have done me good. I therefore confessed myself successively to all the professors; then I amused myself, imagining them turning this horrible secret in their minds. But I could never understand how they could bear the burden of my presence among them and of the vision of all the wrong that I could do.

Nevertheless, on some days I was delightfully worried. I needed this stimulant. I imagined that they would find some way to prevent me from receiving Holy Orders. Then, I redoubled my zeal. My sermons were models, little masterpieces.

I had all the more merit because I had to maintain in addition the good progress of our anti-religious action in the whole world.

Happily, the Uncle had understood that he should not require me to code my work. I only had to furnish one project a week. I overflowed with ideas and this work did not bore me; on the contrary, it was my pleasure and my support.

About the time I was playing with Confession, I was particularly sensitive to one point of doctrine, I mean to say, "the holy virtue of obedience" (as they say). This obedience especially concerns the Pope. I turned this problem over at every angle without being able to understand it.

I was therefore obliged to ask our services to see to it that the confidence shown to the Pope by Catholics be ridiculed discreetly on every possible occasion. I was not unaware that I was asking in this something very difficult. But, all in all, it seemed essential to me to incite Catholics to criticize the Pope.

Someone was charged to watch attentively all the Vatican writings in order to detect even very small details capable of displeasing one category or other of individuals. The quality of those who criticize the Pope does not matter; the only important thing is that he be criticized. The ideal thing, of course, would be that he displeased everybody, that is, reactionaries as well as Modernists.

As to the virtue of obedience, it is one of the principal conventions of this Church.

I thought of weakening it by cultivating remorse. Let everyone imagine himself to be responsible for the actual division of Christianity. Let each Catholic make his *"Mea culpa,"* and try to find out how he could erase four centuries of contempt toward the Protestant sects.

I could help this research by mentioning all that offends Protestants and by suggesting the employment of a little more charity toward them. Charity has this advantage, that we can have it perform any kind of foolishness.

At that time, I still feared that my method might be discovered and that many could notice in it a way of killing God. The subsequent events proved that I was wrong to have that fear. Yet, a French proverb says that "the best is the enemy of good." In this instance, no one ever saw that my fraternal love for the Protestants would lead to destroying all Christianity. I do not wish to say, on the other hand, that Protestants do not have faith (or every sort of differing "faith") and that my services are not concerned about them.

But I rouse them by showing them that they must not convert to Catholicism, that on the contrary, it belongs to the Roman Church to go toward them. Even, at the announcement of the Council (the Council that fills me with joy in advance), I launched a message to all the world which made it gape; it contained an order and a prophecy. First, the prophecy: God Himself, by a great miracle, a miracle altogether spectacular (people revere this) would accomplish the unity of Christians. It is why men should not meddle with it otherwise than by a great openness, a very charitable openness. In other words, Catholics must let go some ballast, in order to allow God to manifest His great miracle in the midst of pure hearts. For Catholics of this time, the pure heart must be he who endeavors, by any means whatsoever, to please Protestants.

The order was also very simple: It was absolutely forbidden for Protestants to convert to Catholicism. And I had this point very much at heart, because conversions had attained an accelerated pace. I had it specified everywhere that the great miracle could not occur if Catholics kept on accepting the conversions of Protestants. I let it be known clearly that God was to be left free in His movements.

And I was listened to and I was followed. I, and not their God, was performing miracles.

I shudder with joy even to this day. This seems to me to have been one of my great successes.

# 8

## *How The Ambitious One Who Thought Himself Stronger Than All Meets "Raven Hair" And Fears His First Weakness*

At the end of two years of seminary life, I was seriously asking myself if I could keep it up.

The will that exercises itself alone is not always sufficient, and I was very young to feed myself only on my hatred.

Nevertheless, I saw this hatred increase; and at first reserved for God, it now extended to all of my surroundings. If only they could have guessed to what degree I hated them all. Even today, I admire myself for having been able to tolerate them. Surely, I am and remain a loner. If sociability is not indispensable to me, on the other hand, a small oasis of human warmth was lacking in my youth. In fact, I had only my professor of singing, whom I visited every Saturday. On certain matters we

54

understood each other without having to spell things out, but he never knew the reality of my mission in all its extensiveness.

The marvelous thing about it was that I could really relax at his house. Without him, I might not have had the strength to resist.

Happily, this writing will never be published, for it is not a good example to my comrades.

I had also received the order to accept certain invitations to worldly affairs. They came to me without my knowing why and how they reached me. I was therefore obliged to obey. I never dared, when I wrote to the Uncle, to ask of him the value of these deeply frivolous occupations.

Anyway, he knew my disgust for this kind of thing, and he already had told me that it would do me some good to know the ways of the world. Let us admit that, but I never made any useful discovery there.

One evening, I was assisting at a grand reception that was particularly brilliant. My gaze fell upon the profile of a young girl, and, suddenly, all that surrounded her vanished, my own senses included.

She had a long neck, more slanting than the tower of Pisa, a very large and black hairdo that I would have liked to dishevel, and a childlike and at the same time wilfull profile. I looked at her breathlessly.

It was as if the two of us were alone, although she did not see me. I was yelling at her interiorly to turn her head around a little, in order that I could steal a look at her, but she did not do so. I do not know how long my ecstasy lasted, but I was brought back to earth by an unknown young man. He had understood all, maybe better than I did. He was good-hearted, since he said to me: "Do you wish me to introduce you to Miss X?" He knew me by name, but mistook me for a university student. In all this social life, no one could recognize me as a seminarian.

A little later, this obliging young man introduced me to "Raven Hair." (I will never give her another name).

I had recovered my calm, thanks to a discreet breathing exerice.

Nevertheless, I was now a different man, totally different. One hundredth of a second had sufficed.

During the evening, I did not try to understand what was happening to me. I was too busy enjoying those new feelings.

I spoke with "Raven Hair" for a few moments, moments during which I could not "eat" her all up, because what was dominating my inner self was the desire to take this young girl all for myself and to hide her in a small house, far from all, a little house in which she would promise to wait for me. She had very large dark eyes that looked at you with an embarrassing seriousness.

And when she was invited to dance, I had to hold both my hands behind my back in order not to kill the one who took her away from me.

Dancing is a diabolical invention. I do not understand how a man can tolerate his wife dancing with another man.

I looked at her waltzing; her dress was marvelous, but my eyes were as if hypnotized by her bent neck, which seemed to present itself to the axe of an executioner.

I do not know why this young girl seemed destined to die a violent death. This feeling increased the fury with which I would have liked to snatch her away from all those people.

What was she doing in the midst of all these fools? What was her occupation in life?

I must succeed in getting her to wish nothing else but to wait for me. Any means would be good to attain this end. She belonged to me, that's all.

But she left with an aged couple whom I did not know. How could I manage to see her again?

She did not pay attention to me, only maybe at the last second when her look met mine.

What did this look mean? Can you find out how to meet me again?...Maybe...in any case, I did not bother any further about what she could think. I had taken the decision of directing her thoughts because I considered that she belonged to me forever.

That she would not agree to that would only be an amusing challenge.

I knew her name and nothing else, I entrusted my singing professor with the task of finding her.

This affair seemed to amuse him considerably. He even said to me, "So you are becoming more human?" I could not understand what he found to be inhuman in me, and I was somewhat vexed by what he had said. He did not want to explain himself. His efforts were lengthy and I had to calm myself down by working with a tenfold zeal.

It was during those days that I launched on the market (we could almost say) the program that would allow Catholics to be accepted by Protestants.

Catholics had hoped too much for the return

of Protestantism to the fold of the Mother Church. It was time that they should lose their arrogance. Charity made it a duty for them. When charity is at stake—I pretended, laughing up my sleeve— nothing wrong can happen.

I prophesied with assurance—so that this would be repeated in the same tones—the suppression of Latin, of priestly vestments, of statues and images, of candles and prie-dieu (so that they could kneel no more).

And I also started a very active campaign for the suppression of the Sign of the Cross. This Sign is practiced only in Roman and Greek Churches. It is time that the latter take notice that they offend other people, who have as many qualities and as much holiness as they have. This Sign, and also genuflections, are all ridiculous customs.

I also prophesied (and we were then in 1940) the disappearance of altars, replaced by a completely bare table, and also of all the crucifixes, in order that Christ be considered as a man, not as a God. I insisted that Mass be only a community meal, to which all would be invited, even unbelievers. And I came to the following prophecy: Baptism for the modern man has become ridiculously magical. Whether given by immersion or not, Baptism must be abandoned in favor of an adult religion.

I searched for the means of suppressing the

Pope, but I could not find the possibility of doing so.

As long as we would not say that the play on words of Christ, "Thou art Peter, and upon this rock I will build My Church, and the gates of Hell shall not prevail against it," was invented by a zealous Roman (but how can we prove that—it is not enough that this were possible), a Pope would always be in power.

I consoled myself by hoping that we would surely succeed in making him look foolish.

The important thing was to cry out against him every time that he started something new and even when he revived old customs too hard to be followed.

Moreover, all that is permitted among Protestants, even if only in one sect, must be authorized among Catholics, that is, the remarriage of divorcees, polygamy, contraception and euthanasia.

The universal Church, having to accept all religious and even the unbelieving philosophers, it was urgent that Christian churches should give up their own proprieties. So I asked them to perform an immense cleaning out.

All that excited heart and mind to worship an invisible God must be unmercifully suppressed.

One must not believe that I ignored, as do some whom I will not name, the power of gestures and of all that speaks to the senses.

A thoughtful mind would have noticed that I was suppressing all that is lovable in a religion which is, on the other hand, quite strict.

To leave them severity was a nice enough trick. I would secretly insinuate that this cruel God might, after all, be a human invention—a God cruel enough to send His only Son to be crucified!!! But I had to be careful that my hatred did not appear in my writings.

As I was overjoyed with these orders and prophecies, my singing professor had me called on the phone. He had found her and was inviting me that same evening to a concert where I could see her again.

Happily, I easily got permission to go out. I had a very nice voice and churchmen were always lenient toward musicians.

I saw her again—more beautiful than the first time—so beautiful, so beautiful—how not to become crazy?

She readily consented to come for a cup of tea on the following Saturday at the house of my singing professor.

I pretended to reside at a University Center. My singing professor bore the name of Achille and he asked me to call him Uncle Achille.

I understand that he wished thereby to give me the illusion of having a family. But I was not very grateful to him for that because his attitude revealed to me that he hoped to see me think seriously of getting married.

How could he have such absurd thoughts? It was a sign that he felt my lack of a priestly vocation, but had absolutely not guessed the power and seriousness of my socialist vocation.

To think of it, I saw that this incomprehension, a sign of my strength of character and of the quality of my dissimulation, could only favor my designs. To be a really great man, it is very advantageous to appear to be ordinary and even dumb. Those who show off before crowds are not those who really pull the strings.

My "Raven Hair" seemed to enjoy herself at Uncle Achille's house. I displayed all the charms of my Slav temperament. Nobody had taught me that little game, but I found out that it was instinctive.

I must say that I took great pride in it.

The woman of my dreams wore, on that day,

a very simple blue dress and had around her neck just one jewel, a large medal of the Virgin, called the Miraculous Medal.

My eyes kept returning all the time to that object and were scorched by it; I would have liked to snatch it away from her and to throw it out the window.

# 9

## *How An Anti-religious Zeal Would Like to Drag "Raven Hair" In Its Wake*

I had to face the truth, I was simply in love for the first time; in love like a poor chap whose intelligence does not dominate his instincts. I saw only one remedy: an always greater zeal for the defense and the advancement of the great cause of the proletariat. It was at that time that I launched the grand campaign of Biblical dialogue. It aimed at arousing Catholics to an assiduous and thoughtful reading of God's word, insisting fully on the freedom of examination practiced by Protestants for four centuries.

I showed that this liberty had given us many generations of truly adult beings and masters of their lives. By these very pious means, I excited Catholics, therefore, to throw off the yoke of papism and the Protestants to become the masters of this new generation.

Although I gave to Protestants the dominating position, I also weakened them, without giving their pride the liberty to guess it. This weakening would come naturally from the emulation of diverse sects.

In this contest, the Catholics could not act the part of arbitrator, because they would be preocuppied only by the desire of reforming themselves.

It was child's play to persuade them that they must implement a return to the sources and a brilliant modernization. I suggested that the zeal to give us, in all languages, new Biblical translations in modern style must not be slowed down. There also, I noted a lively competition. I did not mention the financial aspect of the problem, but the number of translations allowed us to notice that this aspect had not escaped the vigilance of Churchmen.

The modernization of God's Word often allowed the Church's obstinacy to diminish. And that was done in a very natural way.

Every time that a word seemed rarely used and risked not being understood, it was replaced by a word altogether simple—and, of course, always to the detriment of the real meaning. How could I complain about this?

Besides, these new translations facilitated the Biblical dialogue upon which we laid great hope.

For this dialogue would lead to sending Church-men somewhere else, anywhere, so as to let laymen be at liberty to act as adults. I also proposed inter-confessional Biblical meetings. This was my real aim, and moreover it could even go further, by adding a benevolent examination of the Koran and of some other oriental books. To forget "Raven Hair," I personally prepared many sessions of Biblical dialogue by stressing the diverse aspects of some key problems.

One of my preferred dialogues concerned the Pope, because this personage is really an obstacle for me. When I say "this personage," I mean also the texts upon which his title is based. Those texts are also as embarrassing for me as they are for the separated Christians (as they say).

I am very grateful to the one who thought that the word "prevail" has become incomprehensible to modern man and has replaced it by "be able."

Instead of "the gates of Hell will never prevail against it" (the Church), he has written: "The gates of Hell will never be able to do anything against it." This makes my Biblical dialogue meetings much easier, at least in French-speaking countries.

Everyone notices very quickly that this prophecy, which claims that Hell can do nothing against the Church, is absolutely false, and every-one breathes easier because thus vanishes this age-old belief in a divine protection which would definitely always favor the efforts of Catholics (and by implication: never those of heretics!).

I like to launch my dialogues in the labyrinth of the Old Testament. The Book of Genesis, all by itself, is enough to make an honest man become crazy. The older I grow, the more I notice that only the faith of the coalman and the faith of a child can survive in a world in which intelligence takes priority over anything else.

I even have reason to ask this question: "Are there any more coalmen, and above all, are there any more children?"

It seems today, at least in the white race, that childhood dies at birth and is replaced, I must say, by small, quite annoying adults.

I do not know if I must rejoice over this. That faith loses ground by it is all right, but will my faith gain anything by it?

Many question marks arise here.

Not long after my third meeting with "Raven Hair," France, her country, was invaded by Hitler's soldiers and seemed to have put up only an imaginary resistance.

On this occasion, I wrote a very nice letter

to my proud girlfriend, in which I tried to console her.

She agreed to take a ride with me in the country. She had an automobile that her uncle had lent her. In fact, she was staying at the home of a brother of her father. But her real family had remained in France, right in the occupied zone.

She would have liked to return to her country, a very human reaction which pleased me very much. I liked this pride and this need to excel. How I would have wanted to have her become my colleague!

Nevertheless, I dared not come to the problem of faith, nor even to political problems. The medal that she still wore today, on this fourth meeting, put a whole world between us two.

While we were having tea in a charming establishment, which seemed reserved to lovers, a couple made us a little sign of discreet friendship, which filled me with anxiety. The man was the brother of a classmate of mine. I had been invited into his family, and he knew me well. How could he forget that I was a seminarian? I could not hope that much. The young girl in his company was a cousin of "Raven Hair."

I was furious and my girlfriend noticed it. She offered to introduce me to her uncle and aunt, so that I could quietly and naturally visit her at her home, or rather, their home. I thought of asking her, "Under what title?" As betrothed?. . . How could I tell her that I wanted her all for myself, but that I would never marry her? No, I was riveted to Catholic celibacy in order to serve the cause of the proletariat.

If she could have understood my aspiration, it would have been marvelous, but I dared not even to broach the problem to her. And yet, I could then have gone to visit her at her residence. It would have been sufficient that she accept an obscure part.

She noticed that I was not enthusiastic over the idea of being introduced to her family, and she left offended by that. It was not a first quarrel, but a first serious misunderstanding. I did not have enough money to rent an apartment, nor even a studio. The Party would not allow such squandering because it is a grievous bourgeois defect.

On that day we almost separated coldly. Both of us felt that some unknown forces were leagued against us and our newborn love. There was no need of talking to feel that. Moreover, I was asking myself if, like other young girls, she were only prompted by the desire to get married. A legitimate desire, of course, and I did not reproach her for it, but on this occasion, a very disastrous one. I therefore bid her farewell with subtle coldness and without having foreseen the next meeting.

She replied with a slight shrug and walked slowly away.

I remained without stirring, my eyes resting upon her white neck, which bent under the weight of her too-heavy hair—and also her too-sad thoughts. As I remained motionless, she turned around and looked at me. About ten meters separated us. Then I saw this marvelous thing: she was returning— very slowly, her eyes on my eyes, she was returning, she was returning to me. When she was very close to me, she lifted her hands slowly and laid them on my shoulders. She kept on looking at me, and I did not move. Then she continued her gesture by touching my lips with her lips. It was the first time that I kissed a woman.

# 10

## *How A Simple Medal Is Allowed To Play A Part As If It Had Some Kind Of Right Over The Men Whom It Encounters*

Happily, at the very beginning I had rented a post office box, of which Uncle Achille had the key. A post office is very useful when one refuses, without seeming to do so, to give one's real address.

A few days after this kiss, the memory of which would wake me up every night, I received a marvelous letter from "Raven Hair." She wrote to me: "So that I may continue to paint seriously, my uncle has rented a small shop for me. I am expecting you to come there and have tea with me Saturday."

At that time, I quit singing and passed all my Saturdays at her shop. My girlfriend even made a portrait of me. To tell the truth, I must say that she had a real talent and that I was filled with pride by the masterful way with which she had represented my personality. In that portrait I could better find out what I was for her. Without lying, I was much more, in her eyes, than a charming prince. I was more of a conqueror, more manly. . . with maybe a secret inkling of cruelty. I asked her how she saw my character and if she really suspected me of having secret and quite disturbing defects.

She seemed to become indignant over this. I told her, "Yet, this portrait reveals a conquering, a proud spirit with a secret sparkle of cruelty." She was dumbfounded and told me that I had too much imagination and that, on the contrary, she had wanted to represent what I was for her, that is, the ideal man. . .and how could an ideal man have secret defects? I then asked her what were my apparent defects, since I had no secret ones. She replied to me with a bewildering foresight that it was a certain taste for the "ivory tower."

To gain her forgiveness, I assured her, and it was the real truth, that she was always with me in my "ivory tower." She answered me that she had no doubt about that, but that it was a presence that I alone could perceive and that she could feel only an absence. How to conciliate my desire to have her all to myself and that of not being able to be everything to her?

She asked me what obstacle prevented me from being receptive and open. I hesitated a long while,

and I decided to risk everything with her by point-
ing at the medal that she wore on her neck. She
looked at me with great surprise. "Don't you have
the Faith?" she asked simply. I said, "No," without
adding anything else.

She implored me to explain the effect that the
medal produced on me. I answered her, "It is an
obstacle in the sense that it represents something
which we will never be able to love together." While
she was thinking this over, I insisted, saying: "Moreover, it seems on purpose to come between us two
in order that we might never belong to one another."
Then she took off the medal and gave it to me.
I put it in my pocket, asking myself what I would
do with it. I believe it was made of gold. I would
have liked to have it melted and to have something
else engraved on it, but this was impossible.

By this gesture she had united our two desti-
nies in a very strange manner. She was tactful
enough not to ask me what I was going to do with
it. In the following days I had some anxiety about
this subject. I had the temptation to get some information about this thing, which bore the qualifier
"miraculous," not that I could believe that this orna-
ment had the power to perform miracles. According to me, nobody performs miracles. Those that
are narrated as such are either invented or will later
be scientifically explained. Nevertheless, I read that
this medal was reputed to have brought back
unbelievers to the Faith. I did not believe in the

reality of this fact, nor even, of course, in its possibility, but I feared that my dear friend had this hope in her heart, which destroyed for me the gesture of giving it to me, of sacrificing the medal for me. On the contrary, in this new light, she had not made a sacrifice. Was I stupid to such a degree? Was it not also stupidity to be tormented about this? A few months later, while we were both bent over her latest sketches, in front of a wood fire fostering calmness, I softly asked her this question: Had she not given me her medal in the hope of converting me; was it not just the opposite of a sacrifice? She snuggled in my arms and answered me: "I never lie; surely I want that medal to bring about your conversion. I ask that favor every night and morning, my poor Dear, and also many times a day, maybe at every quarter of an hour." I did not know what to answer.

I feared nothing from this medal and her prayers; for me they were mere childishness; nevertheless, I suffered as if I had been defeated. For, on my part, I wanted her, with all my strength, as my colleague, and without the medal. What was it between us? The more I thought it out, the more I saw the logic that the man should win, at least in such a strong and burning love like ours. But I said no such thing. Nevertheless, I knew that she could not be all mine until she thought like I did.

It was not a matter of pride but because I had to explain to her why I could not marry her. If she had shared my ideas and had been willing to help me in my mission, she would have acceded, I think, to living with me very secretly in a marital way. Not only could I never get married, but I must also appear to be altogether virtuous.

One winter evening, while I was drawing the curtains and she was serving tea, I thought that I had pricked myself with a pin forgotten in the tassel. I looked more closely and found that it was a very small medal, of white metal, I suppose of which the rather coarse ring had a defect which pricked. It was the same kind of a medal, only much smaller.

When I turned around, she was watching me. She had understood. "So the curtain also needs to be converted?" said I with bitterness. "Don't be absurd and mean," she answered me. "It is just because I am not absurd that I wish to understand what you expect from this talisman." She became angry and her face turned completely red. "It is not a talisman." "Then what is it?" "An act of Faith." "A Faith in what?" "Not in what; in whom . . . in Her, the Mother of Jesus Christ." (If I use capital letters, it is because she spoke with capital letters).

I did not wish to continue this useless conversation; I remained silent. She kept on talking in very low tones: "One must believe that metal, wood or paper has not the least importance. I know that it is this aspect of the issue which appalls you. In fact, a medal is only a simple way of exteriorizing one's faith, and not only of exteriorizing it, but also of increasing it. The fact of always carrying this medal on myself and of having it in the house where I work incites me to pray more often to her who gave me Jesus Christ."

Thus she had not really sacrificed her medal for me. She possessed many others. I do not know what prevented me from raping her at that very moment. She will never know how close she came to it. There followed a lengthy silence. I was trembling with anger. I would have liked to cry out my hatred. But I only said, "You are mine and I cannot tolerate that you love something more than you love me." "How strange you are! These two cannot be compared. All that is religious belongs to another domain. It is neither a matter of intelligence, nor heart." "Then, what is it?" I asked with impatience. She answered softly, "The immense domain of the Supernatural." "I know nothing about it." "I thought so," she said with her smile, which I cannot resist. Is she aware that she dominates me solely by her smile?

At certain moments it seems that there is nothing but this strange power over me. Her smile is slow. One has time to see it come. Her lips open with much softness and such slowness that each time one asks himself if it will develop fully. When the brightness of her teeth appears, one feels filled with joy, as in my case. I then abandon myself to the benefit of this delightful tenderness. It is what I did at this moment when I needed a quieting comfort.

Then she asked me the strangest question of all. She said to me, "Why do you not want to marry me?" I had never said that I did not want to marry her. But "Raven Hair" seemed to possess a certain gift of divination, a gift that sometimes scares me. What did she really know about me? I answered her: "I do not wish to get married, but I cannot tell you why." She let out a little sigh and said to me, "Is it because I believe in God?" Women are strange; they can pass from childishness to divination. My mother was like that. I answered, "A couple must love the same things. It is in fact the greatest obstacle." She smiled again and said, "I will never love anyone but you."

# 11

## *How The Destructive Work Seems To Make Great Progress Although It Runs Against Ridiculously Childish Obstacles*

At that time, I showed great energy in destroying the Marian cult. I insisted greatly upon the difficulty that Catholics and the Orthodox caused Protestants by keeping up their numerous devotions to the Virgin Mary. I pointed out that the dear Separated Brethren were more logical and wiser. This human creature, about whom we know almost nothing, becomes in our Church in some way more powerful than God (or, at least, more gentle). On this account, I defended the rights of God with much amusement. I stressed the fact that many Protestants believe that Mary had other children after Jesus. Do they believe that her virginity was safeguarded at the birth of this First Child? This is difficult to say. But, in all this, it is hard to determine the exact beliefs of these different branches of Christianity. In fact, each one believes what he wishes. Nevertheless, it is relatively easy to know what they dislike.

I therefore advocated the suppression of the Rosary and of the numerous feast days reserved to Mary. My missal numbered twenty-five of them. To these may be added certain regional feasts. And, also included in my project, is the total destruction of medals, images and statues. Much work in sight, but it was worthwhile.

But, I did not see how I would be able to suppress Lourdes and Fatima—and some other pilgrimage places of minor importance. As for Lourdes, it is terribly annoying; it is an open wound in the hearts of Protestants. Never could the Universal Church take root as long as this place of pilgrimage would every year draw several million individuals of all races. I made a special study of the Lourdes phenomenon, but this extensive undertaking did not lead to much discovery—just enough to show that there was a serious enough difference between primitive testimonies.

One spoke of Bernadette's fainting and of being pursued by the apparition up to the place where she was residing—a mill, if my memory is correct. The other denied this fact. The child herself did not acknowledge it. One could say that she had forgotten it, but this did not appear to be serious. I detest propaganda that is based on lies. I know very well that the Party approves lying when a greater welfare is at stake, but for my part, I prefer dignity. I thus feel stronger. I even feel that I exceed those of my Party who have made use of lies. I believe that it is always possible to succeed by only playing with truth. It is sufficient to know how to interpret the useful aspect of each truth. Thus, I may say that my mission has its foundation on this command of Christ: "Love one another." Simply, I was directing the charitable regard of the whole Church for the branches of Christianity deemed heretical. By listening to me, they disobeyed the Apostles, but in general, they took no notice of this.

Another difficulty was that, to dethrone Mary, it was necessary to suppress Christmas. But Christmas has become a feast of joy, even for unbelievers. The latter cannot even explain why and how it is so. It has to be noted that peace and joy are very desirable, good things. On the other hand, it is consoling to note that if Jesus of Nazareth is not the Son of God, His Mother is of no importance. It is not even worthwhile to know her name.

And for him who wishes to keep on admiring, with just reason, the greater part of the moral teaching of Jesus (whom I accuse of being revolutionary), it becomes ridiculous to venerate the childhood of the said Jesus. What is this little baby born in a manger? What does it change? It is to be noted that, whereas Protestant Christians do not believe generally the virginal birth of the Prophet Jesus, seven hundred million Moslems have adopted this dogma through their Koran. Which, we must realize, obliges half of humanity to venerate this young woman. Surely something very odd... Nevertheless, the oddest thing is the fact that Moslems consider Jesus only as a Prophet, and a lesser Prophet than their Mohammed, who was born in an altogether natural way.

Human oddness has no limit. All this strengthens my conviction that to deny the virginity of Mary is the safest way to transform Christians into disciples of a man who would not at all be God. Who does not see how useful it is to kill Jesus of Nazareth before killing God?

The Gospels and Epistles, in fact the whole New Testament, become the word of man, and of course, each one could chose in them what he wishes, criticize what displeases him and deny what is exaggerated... Such is our goal. Whereas in the Orient icons represent the principal devotion to Mary and are today in all of Russia hidden or destroyed, in the Occident the Rosary is very popular. This devotion, which professes to honor fifteen so-called Mysteries, must be vigorously destroyed. It is capable, all by itself, of maintaining and propagating the faith in a Triune God.

As for all other things, it will be necessary to make all those who keep on reciting the Rosary feel guilty.

Such is the summary of the orders which I sent throughout the world at the time when, in my seminarian's room, I had hung up on the picture of the one I could never marry, the medal spoken of as miraculous. Anybody would have thought that I was asking for a miracle; whereas instead, I wanted to fortify myself in my hatred, which however was not petty.

On the following Saturday, "Raven Hair" could not receive me; they had just gone on a Marian pilgrimage. My anger was equalled only by my amusement, for surely it was for my conversion that the poor little girl had gone to all this trouble. I went to exercise my voice, which I had neglected to do these last weeks. My friend Achille was altogether delighted. I could not refrain from telling him the whole story about the medal. I was dumbfounded by his answer. He told me, "Beware! All that is said about that medal is true. If you have it in your room, you are in danger." I asked him if he had a fever. He pretended not to hear, but the very sight of this medal made him sick and he could never bear its presence without becoming wild. The human heart is an incomprehensible chasm. That my old professor—an ardent Communist—could speak in such a manner worried me greatly. For the first time in my life, I had doubts about the success of my mission. I felt frightfully unhappy, and I then stopped to think that this work was my only reason for living, my only love. I knew it theoretically, but on this day, I learned it in the suffering of my mind, disgusted by the stupidity of man's heart.

I wanted to discuss it with him, but to no avail. Achille answered me: "I believe in nothing—neither in God, nor in the devil, much less in the Virgin Mary—but I am afraid of that medal; that's all." "But, do you believe that it could convert you?" I cried out, shaking him by the shoulders. He said to me, "Surely not, but I'm afraid; that's all." "But do you not see the stupidity of this fear? Don't you see that it would be honorable for you to overcome this childish fear by placing this medal prominently in your house?" He did not answer, so I insisted. With weariness, he said to me, "Let's talk about something else." "No, I will pursue this matter to the end, for it is the future of humanity which is at stake in what you believe to be only childishness. What will become of Communists if, like you, they remain secretly terrorized by an icon or a medal? What will they become? Think."

He did not want to think. It was therefore up to me to do so in his stead, because for me it will always be impossible to remain passive in the face of defeat. Every difficulty excites me and is stimulating to me.

In the face of his obstinacy, I left, slamming the door, but I knew very well what I was going to do.

On the following Saturday, before going to visit "Raven Hair," I went by Achille's house with a hammer, a nail, the medal and its chain. Without allowing him to discuss it, I went straight to his bedroom. I hammered the nail at the head of his bed, where the crucifix is often placed, and I hung on it the Miraculous Medal.

The following Saturday, Achille had moved away, and I never knew what had become of him.

This disappearance was a great inconvenience for my activities, at least until Achille could be replaced. Upon leaving, he had returned to me the medal and also the key to the post office box.

# 12

## *The Catechism Of The Year 2000 And A Poor But Zealous Student*

During that year, I worked hard on the composition of a new catechism which would suit the Universal Church, such as I wanted to see established in the whole world. Shaping the minds of young children is a vital necessity for all doctrine that has self-respect. To teach atheism from the outset of childhood is important because the mysterious part of religious doctrine leaves a certain nostalgia, except in truly superior beings, to whom I belong. But it would not be honest on my part to deny that many atheists are not altogether frank with themselves. No one likes to acknowledge his weaknesses; it is why one must endeavor never to be weak. Moreover, the strong must give to the weak—who are a majority—a solid support which can prevent them from tripping. In the light of religious doctrines, it is wise to consider each man as handicapped, at least to the end of this twentieth century.

It is altogether reasonable to hope that the cure will be at hand for the year 2000. A certain number of words must be banished completely from the human vocabulary, and the best method is to be sure that children never hear these words.

That is why it is much better to compose a new catechism than to hope for a simple suppression of all religious teaching . . . No, this will be possible only in two or three generations.

For the moment, one must play with the phenomenon that "Church" equals the "Meeting of friendly brethren of the whole world." This catechism will therefore be one of that friendship which will replace the antiquated Christian charity.

The word "charity" must absolutely be banished and be replaced by the word "love," which allows you to keep your feet on the ground and even to play all kinds of ambiguous games without seeming to do so.

I must say that I have always had and continue to have great respect for the underlying and even subterranean power of ambiguous interaction when it is in hands worthy of it.

While I was preparing this new catechism, I took note of all that must be gradually modified or suppressed in the actual teaching. I also felt the burning desire to have "Raven Hair" share my convictions. It was she who made it easy for me, by describing to me her pilgrimage and the so-called "miracles" performed by the Holy Virgin Mary.

I explained to her that all these religious phenomena, whatever they are in reality, were the fruit of her own creation. She vehemently denied this. I said to her: "All that you can neither see nor feel is the result of your creation, and I do not understand why this angers you." "You do not see it because you do not know that my entire faith has been revealed to me and comes from Heaven. I would have been completely incapable of inventing all that." "You have not invented this yourself; that is true, but you are imitating your ancestors; that's all." "No," she told me, "it is more than an imitation." I calmly explained to her that, for example, her belief in the Real Presence of Jesus Christ in the Eucharist produces this presence according to the strength of her faith, but for anyone who believes in nothing, nothing is produced. She would not admit this and, on the other hand, it was important for me that, following the example of Protestants, she should take this course. The real aim that I took pains to hide from her was the suppression of all faith, but before that I had to have her go through this intermediate stage. I proved to her by the Gospels, and especially by the cures effected by Christ for which the faith of the sick person is always required, that this said faith was in reality what performed the cure. But she was as stubborn as a child, pretending that Christ had wanted to arouse faith, this being a greater blessing than a corporal cure. I explained to her that nothing religious exists outside of creative faith, and that is why it is absurd to baptize babies, that we should wait until they come of age, and that Baptism could be suppressed someday as a magical action of a rather childish past.

She started to cry and told me that we should stop meeting for awhile. I agreed willingly to this because I had in fact much to do and I thought, moreover, that a separation might render her more docile, because women do not bear grief as well as we men do.

As for me, I was too much attached to her and I was proud to prove my strength of character. I obtained permission to follow two courses at the University, which allowed me to introduce myself in that circle without revealing my being a seminarian.

The Director had authorized me to dress in lay clothes every time that I thought it necessary. He seemed even to admit that the cassock had become anachronistic. We understood each other almost without speaking, knowing very well that the modern priest would be altogether different from his predecessors.

It is a truism to repeat that one must be in accord with his time. For my part, I figured then that the Church was quite backward. To me it seemed easy to prove that since the Council of Trent it had not moved forward at all and that it should therefore make up for lost time.

I was also obliged to replace Achille, because I could not myself go to the post office box and I could not code my correspondence either. I did not have time to do it. I needed a reliable man, and in time of war it was hard to find one. At last I received the order to contact a professor of the University, which at first sight seemed to be a practical move. But when I saw the old fellow, I was disgusted. I have a sure flair for judging people. This one reeked of treason. I nevertheless gave him the key to the post office box, but decided to refer the matter to higher authority before giving him works to be coded. Unhappily, I received the order to obey without discussion.

I worried very much over this, and I decided to find a second correspondent to whom I would entrust the same work; thus, it would be easy, at least after the war, to make comparisons.

I almost came to the point of hoping that my suspicions would be right, first of all for the pleasure of being right, but especially to compare the worth of my two correspondents to whom I would entrust two different texts on the same subject and bearing the signature AA-1025. If the professor were a traitor, he had to be careful to introduce very prudent transformations to my texts, unless he thought that he could take advantage of the war to destroy all my work. Whatever the case, I had good reason to hire a second correspondent.

I found him among the poor students. He was a bit hot-headed, but his zeal suited me. I let him understand that he might hope to have a bright future with us. It is not the custom of the Party to excite the egotism and avarice of man, but I had to see to it that a sensible calmness should develop in this young man. When I was through settling this matter, I was strongly tempted to see "Raven Hair" again. I cared too much. This was not fitting for a militant Communist, still less for a future Grand Chief of the Party. I had already gone through three years of seminary life; only three more remained. After that, everyone agreed that I would be sent to Rome to undertake higher studies. Then I think I would myself become a professor, probably a professor in a seminary.

Those are key positions in the Church which afford one the possibility of forming patiently an altogether new clergy who will have nothing in common with the old one, except the name.

My life was already all mapped out for me, and I did not desire another one. But I must admit to myself that a particle of sand, as powerful as a rock, had intruded itself into the gears. If only I had been endowed with a frivolous character, I could have

considered "Raven Hair" as an hygienic pastime.
But I was not even her lover. I did not want to
be, as long as she did not share my dearest convictions. For me, the union of man and woman must
be total, or it does not exist. Only the union of
hearts and minds can allow the union of bodies;
otherwise, it is prostitution.

I found myself to be in the following absurd
position—to be the man who was endeavoring to
destroy all religions on earth and to be unable to
convince a young girl twenty years old. I knew that
I should leave her. I did not forget that the Uncle,
in his Russia which was at war, would not be happy
if he knew all this. And I also thought that I was
not watched so closely as in time of peace.

But the height of my distress was that there
was something that I had not the courage to do.

# 13

## *How The Apostles' Creed And The Seven Sacraments Are Severely Censured*

While working on my new catechism, which could be called *Catechism of the Religion of Man,* I noticed that it would be a wise thing to prepare a series, portioning out each time the modifications and restrictions, in order that minds would gradually get used to it. The first edition must modestly suppress two articles of the Apostles' Creed.

First, to replace the word "Catholic" by "Universal," which means the same thing. But it is very important that this word "Catholic" should not offend Protestant ears and would not incite the faithful of the Roman Rite to believe themselves to be Super-Christians.

Afterwards, to bluntly suppress the cult of the Saints. The Saints must disappear before God does, although it is much easier to kill God than His Saints. For the time being, I would proceed as follows: First, suppress all the Saints who have not been formally approved and also those who did not have significant success. Suppress also all those who helped to fight against the Reform, because they have nothing to do with our present epoch, in which Unity concerns all hearts.

Later, it would be particularly crafty to demand discreetly, with great emotion and crocodile tears, the rehabilitation, then the beatification, and even the canonization of the greatest heretics, especially those who have shown a burning, a devouring and explosive hatred toward the Church of Rome. It will be better at first to launch a few "trial balloons" with Luther, for example; and if there is no reaction on the part of Catholics—I mean, if they are not offended—then this aspect of our activities will play a little solo, with prudence and modesty, at regular intervals, and then increasingly more frequently. Next, we will proceed to suppress Judgment, Heaven, Purgatory and Hell. That is even easier.

Many are well disposed to believe that the goodness of God surpasses every offense. All we have to do is to insist on this goodness. A God whom no one fears quickly becomes a God about whom no one thinks. Such was the end to be reached.

After this, the Ten Commandments of God could be kept, but the Six Commandments of the Church should be suppressed. They are ridiculous...ridiculous...

———————

*Here, I allow myself to interrupt Michael's memoirs, because I feel too much like speaking. I do not know what the Editor will think of it. Maybe he will take a big red pencil and, while crossing out my impertinent reflections, he will say to himself: "Does this woman without talent imagine that I will let her put her two cents in the very middle of a text that does not belong to her?" That is what probably will happen, and no one will ever know but myself.*

*But if the red pencil has not yet been put to work, I must say that I feel responsible for this publication and that the Six Commandments of the Church, which have been taken away from us under pretext of giving us the noble liberty of sanctifying ourselves according to our tastes, also carry a heavy responsibility, if I am allowed thus to express myself. I do not like to complain, I do not like those who are satisfied to moan, and I do not like those who have the soul of a slave (that is, I only mean to say that I am not attracted by that kind of people), but the Six Commandments of the Church were our friends. To believe that we obeyed them just because we thought that by doing so we would automatically gain an eternity of supernatural happiness is surely almost insulting.*

*But I, who am only a mere nurse, accustomed to remain silent, would like to say the same thing, that the clergymen of this century try to make them-selves disagreeable. Why?. . .it is something that I cannot guess.*

*But it is a universally known fact that they are endeavoring to impose upon us their innovations, as if the latter came from their purely supernatural love for their very dear and beloved faithful.*

*Thus, we the faithful, the lambs, would have felt secret grief on seeing our dear priests exercising their ministry at the foot of a high altar, with this (for us), that worsening circumstance that they turned their backs toward us.*

*It is strange, but they never guessed that we knew perfectly well that they were speaking to God— in our name, of course. No, they were moved (not only women are artful) by our isolation and our secret griefs, so they first came down to the level of the communion table, and this only on great feast days.*

*The result was that, on those days, only the first four rows could see something. And it is then, and only then, that all the other rows felt abandoned.*

*After this, they put up an ordinary table at the foot of the altar steps, and the former high altar quickly became a vestige of a childish past and so showy that it must be destroyed—in this century in which man is about to be deified.*

Because the Blessed Sacrament could not be kept on a table, they relegated it generally to an opening rapidly carved in one of the side walls of the church. Sometimes clergymen kept the Blessed Sacrament in what was formerly the Tabernacle, which became a small cupboard stripped of all that surrounded it. Some of them said Mass and performed other ceremonies with their backs turned toward the Blessed Sacrament, something that formerly was strictly forbidden. But they looked at us and we could behold them at our ease, and this was, it seems, much more important, especially when they needed to blow their nose.

On this table—called an altar and about which no one knows if it has been blessed and if it holds the relic of a martyr (as required by a long-standing custom)—they placed a small crucifix.

When they found out that this meek Christ on the cross had his back turned to us and was looking only at them, they suppressed it, as well as the candles and other accessories unworthy of such a scientific century. It is their way of collaboration with what is ordinarily called "mutation," which so designates all changes, noteworthy or not, and thus, by this highly learned denomination, they place these changes on a pedestal, which no one will dare oppose.

By always bending down paternally to our spiritual needs, the clergymen of this century made other discoveries.

*Having noticed that Protestants (to whom they vow special affection) do not kneel in their temples, they concluded that we must desire to do the same, but for a different motive, for we were not yet ripe to cultivate the desire of imitating the Protestants, but that we must certainly wish to be invited to imitate our priests, who do not kneel while celebrating the Mass. Thus they chose a few young colleagues and gave them all authority over us, and also the use of one or several microphones.*

*It was at the time when we had to put up with "Sit-Stand; Sit-Stand" during the whole Mass, as military commands being re-echoed and destroying all desire for a humble and quiet prayer. . ."Sit-Stand," because "one does not come to Mass to pray," they cried out at that time.*

*In ten years, we were well trained and our trainers can now rest.*

*It seems that even they have taken a liking to rest; at least, their last innovations confirm this diagnosis.*

*In the first place, they have multiplied concelebration, in which only one man devotes himself to pronounce all the words of the Mass. In general, he chooses the shortest Canon, out of charity, I believe, toward his colleagues, who are waiting for the word "Amen" with a well-hidden impatience.*

*Since our Masses have now given precedence of honor to the three readings of the Bible, although our culture does not allow us to understand a tenth part of them, they only give to the sacrifice proper (allowing that some of them still believe they are offering a sacrifice) a minimum of time with a maximum of noise.*

*Those concelebrations allow all the other clergymen present, who have quickly passed a white alb over their trousers, their shirts or their blazers, to pronounce only the few words of the Consecration, with outstretched arm (which, I fear, must tire them a little). So these concelebrations enable them to dream during all the rest of the ceremony.*

*To flatter the lay faithful and render them docile to new future innovations, the readings of the Old Testament and of the Epistles are very often performed by some young man, or some prominent person who does not know how to articulate, or even by some pretty young girl with naked thighs.*

*I hope that the Editor and the readers of this book will forgive a nurse, who usually restrains herself, those few lines in which any man with a heart will read the grief which dictated them. Once more, I beg your pardon and I will now allow the secret agent to speak of a cause that tries to push the Barque of Peter to shipwreck.*

Concerning the suppression of the Commandments of the Church, we must praise the Christian
who has become an adult and who knows perfectly
well that God is too immense to be preoccupied
about seeing us eat meat or not on Friday. As to
the annual Confession, it would be a good thing
to replace it by a community ceremony in which
a priest will enumerate the most usual crimes against
the lower classes, because it is toward these sins
that the attention of the people should be drawn.
Private Confession is a waste of time. But on the
contrary, the ceremony that I am dreaming up will
condition minds and will produce excellent fruit.

But this requires a well-trained clergy. As for
the obligatory Mass on Sunday, it will be well to
remark that modern man needs fresh air and green
fields, and that it is altogether desirable that he
go out to the country on Saturday and Sunday.

Thus, those who still care for a cult or a weekly
Mass could be authorized to choose Friday instead
of Sunday. Friday evening would be well-suited,
except for those who leave for the country on that
evening. Then, they would be allowed to choose
Thursday. Finally, what must take priority over anything else is that each one will follow his own
conscience.

This method, invented by Protestants, which

consists in obeying one's conscience, is of great excellence. It does not permit giving orders that will risk displeasing some, and it allows replacing these orders by various suggestions which let freedom act at ease.

Of course, all that concerns supernatural life and grace will have to be suppressed. These are dangerous notions.

Prayer, therefore the *Our Father,* will be momentarily kept. But it will be very clever to oblige Catholics to use familiar language with God, under the charitable pretext of adopting, in all countries, for the translation into the common language a version in accord with that of the Protestants. It will be an amiable manner to obtain forgiveness for four centuries of arrogance.

If these new translations displease older people, as it is easy to foresee, it will be all the better.

Afterwards come the Seven Sacraments, which are all to be revised, all the more so because Protestants only have two. All Christians of all denominations have kept Baptism, but for my part, it is the Sacrament that I would like to see disappear first. This seems relatively easy. It is too childish a Sacrament—almost as childish as the Sign of the Cross and Holy Water.

I would start by deciding that Baptism would

be conferred on adults only, and only on those who believed that they could not do without it. I see all that an intelligent man would derive from this. Truly, I do not know whence comes all that I invent, but I am a man of genius. I feel genius coming out through all the pores of my skin. Of course the idea that Baptism erases Original Sin must be put aside—*that* Sin is a pure literary invention. The story of Adam and Eve must be told, but only to be laughed at: it will be taught that Baptism is simply a sign of belonging to Universal Christianity, that anyone can give it, but that everybody can do without it. We must take advantage of this occasion to sing the praises of the holy souls who live in non-Christian religions. This would make them feel guilty. Excellent idea.

Of course, the Sacrament of Confirmation, which pretends to confer the Holy Spirit and can be administered only by a bishop, must be vigorously suppressed. This attitude will permit denouncing the dogma of the Holy Trinity as offensive to Jews and Moslems, as well as to certain new Protestant Sects.

Therefore, it will not be necessary anymore to consecrate Holy Chrism on Holy Thursday. All this looks too much like magic.

It will be necessary to note that faith can very well survive without ceremonies or other exterior manifestations and that, in this case, it is a nobler faith. We must also insist very much on the eminent virtues that are to be seen among pagans, Jews, Moslems and Communists, because I have often noticed that some Catholics are often ashamed that there are more Saints in their Church than in others.

As for the Sacrament called Penance, it would be replaced by a community ceremony, which will only be an examination of conscience directed by a well-trained priest, all of which would be followed by a general absolution, as in some Protestant Churches.

Modern priests will be rid of the unending hours of confession and of the burden which they represent. While writing this, I cannot prevent myself from thinking about the unhappy seminary professors—who are all dead at the time I write this—and who bore until death, each for himself in the sight of his God, the useless knowledge of the danger that I represented for the future of the Church.

These community confessions could take place twice a year, at Easter and Christmas. Some young priests will be trained by a solid Socialist formation because it will be their aim, in the midst of a detailed examination of social sins, to direct minds toward Marxism.

The motives for contrition will be only the lack of justice toward others. We will have to convince all that the Christian is a man who has confidence in man. Everyone will ask himself this question: "Can others have confidence in me?" God will not be mentioned in this ceremony, which will not be called a Sacrament anymore (because this word must also disappear from the vocabulary). Of course, no one will talk any more about Indulgences. No one will then know the exact meaning of this word. As for the Sacrament of Extreme-Unction, we will have to find another word for it. It will not be possible to suppress it at the very outset of our reform, since it concerns the very sick. Such a measure would not be popular, but we will have to see to it that the notion of eternal life, judgment, Heaven, Purgatory or Hell be replaced by the sole desire to be cured. After a while, people will notice that doctors do not need the help of a priest in his profession of a healer. Nevertheless, I would willingly choose the expression "Sacrament of the sick," and to avoid the idea of eternal life, it would be allowed to offer this Sacrament, even in case of a light illness.

On the other hand, I have no worry over this; all these Sacraments will easily disappear. People have no more time for all those things.

As to the Sacrament of Holy Orders, which confers the power to exercise clerical functions, we will evidently have to keep it. In our Universal Church, we will need priests who will be teachers of some Socialist doctrine.

These priests will be able to establish feasts, using folklore, for example, because people need feasts.

But these feasts will be totally in honor of man, without any reference whatsoever to a god.

Marriage is not a useless Sacrament, under condition that it be only a family feast. We will have to sweep away all those customs which advocate, in some backward countries, that the religious marriage, that is, Catholic, be the only legal form of marriage. No, civil marriage should be the only one required. Thus, this basely authoritative Church will no longer be able to forbid divorce and the remarriage of divorcees.

I know very well that Jesus of Nazareth has spoken in opposition to this opinion, but I have already said elsewhere that we must know what to choose in His teachings that is suitable to modern man.

The indissolubility of marriage also is an obligation which spurns the happiness of man. And those who speak about the welfare of the child ignore that the child will be much better off when it will belong to the State.

And of course marriage will not be refused to the priests who ask for it, not any more than the Sacrament of Holy Orders will be refused to women.

# 14

## *How A Universal Church Should Sing The Glory Of Man*

Before proceeding to a thorough study of the Sacrament of the Eucharist, I sent my work to my student correspondent and also to "Raven Hair."

The student was so enthusiastic about it that he contacted me one day at the University to hand me a series of articles. Blushing, he wanted my support to have them published in a good review. In principle, we should not have talked together in public, but I thought that on account of the war, I could take some initiatives. To speak openly with the student, to exchange documents, presented no danger.

I felt so much at ease that, as soon as I was authorized to follow two courses at the University, I bought myself a motorcycle. I could thus abstain from traveling in the company of one student or another.

The articles of the student were simply remarkable. I could even have become jealous of him because I am not a writer. But I saw at once what an invaluable influence these excellently phrased articles would have.

We were heading for an ideal collaboration; I was producing the ideas, coldly presented in their rigorous logic, and the student chose the most remarkable ones or at least those which would inspire his astute articles. To feel that my ideas were sprouting and would soon bloom in literary flowers excited my genius because, in this tandem, I was the genius, the student was only the talent. I easily found a review that, for a good price, regularly accepted publishing the articles inspired by me. I had them sent to all the countries not at war, in order that they could be translated and circulated. But I must admit that they did not have much success until after the war. Having more confidence in the student than in the professor imposed by my chiefs, I rented a second post office box and gave him the key. As he was well paid, he looked upon me as a god and would have gotten killed for my sake.

Since "Raven Hair" did not answer me, I sent her regularly the student's articles, explaining in a short tender letter that they were the reflection of my thoughts. "Raven Hair" was sensitive to the student's talent and wrote to tell me that his articles were much nicer than my so very blunt work.

I laughed up my sleeve because the articles said nothing else but what I had so brutally enounced. This confirmed my idea that literary talent can help people to swallow all new plans as if they were coated with chocolate.

During all these long weeks, "Raven Hair" did not invite me to return to her shop. I was fuming with rage when one day I met the girl, whom I considered mine, in the corridors of the University. She had decided to follow courses in Ancient Art. She stopped to tell me that she was preparing an answer to my plan for a new catechism, hoping to be able to discuss it with me quietly. To discuss, to discuss. . . I was not in the habit of meeting the least obstacle to the ways in which I launched my ideas. But I answered her that the pleasure of meeting her was so strong in me that I could not refuse her desire to talk. Nevertheless, I promised myself to let her know that a woman who is really in love, even without noticing it, should adopt all the opinions of the man that her heart has chosen.

On that day, I only told her that I was working on the Sacrament of the Eucharist in order to complete the new catechism which I had sent her. She sighed, tears came up to her eyes, and finally she went away without answering me.

I wanted to write, at the beginning of such a thrilling work, the true definition of the Eucharist, I mean the one which is considered the only true

one by Catholics (of course, Protestants have many
others). To the question, "What is the Eucharist?"
every Catholic child must answer thus: "The
Eucharist is a Sacrament that contains really and
substantially the Body, the Blood, the Soul and the
Divinity of Jesus Christ, under the species of bread
and wine." Only that!!! To solve this problem, one
must work seriously. Not that this belief cannot be
opposed, but one must be prudent and not undertake a frontal attack. This so-called "Real Presence
of Christ under the species of bread and wine" must
be attacked indirectly. If you attack it frontally,
Catholics will rebel. Nothing is more dangerous,
for it is well known that persecution strengthens
the Faith. It is therefore necessary not to mention
"Real Presence" and to shed some light on all that
can destroy or weaken this conviction.

It is of prime necessity completely to reform
the words of the Mass, and it will be well even
to suppress the word itself and to replace it by "The
Lord's Supper" or by "Eucharist" (for example).
The Renovation of the Mass must minimize the
importance of what they call "Consecration" and
must give to the Communion a much more trivial
appearance. This is a long-term project, which must
neglect no detail.

Thus, to begin with, it is to be noted that the
priest who offers the Sacrifice turns his back to
the public and seems to speak directly to an Invisible God, a God nevertheless represented by the

large crucifix facing him. This priest is therefore the one chosen by God and, at the same time, the representative of the people who look at him. He gives an impression of strength, but also of separation.

It will be good to make the parishioners feel that they are lost, too much isolated, somewhat abandoned, and that they would be very happy if the priest would get nearer to them.

When this idea will have sufficiently progressed, we will suggest the possibility of abandoning the high altar and of replacing it by a small table, completely bare, where the priest will stand facing the people.

Moreover, the part of the cult which properly concerns the Eucharist and which requires this table, shall be shortened as much as possible, and the part concerning the teaching of the Word of God noticeably increased. It is well known that Catholics are shockingly ignorant of the Bible, so this modification of the Mass will appear justified to them. I do not say that they will be happy to listen to long extracts from the Bible, for very often they will understand nothing, but it is not necessary for them to understand, at least not until truly Socialist priests will have been trained.

Each text forming the Ordinary of the Mass will be carefully compared with the texts used by

the Anglicans and the Lutherans, in order to promote a single text or varying texts apt to be accepted
by these three religions.

Who does not see the great advantage there
is in this process, which will give very opposite
meanings to the same words? Thus, the unity of
minds will be accomplished in ambiguity, for it cannot be done otherwise. There is no other alterna-
tive: conversion or ambiguity. I choose this expedient
which allows one to do away with the "Real
Presence."

When Catholics will see Protestants receive
Communion at their Masses, without having been
converted, they will no longer have confidence in
their ancient "Real Presence." It will be explained
to them that this Presence only exists insofar as
it is believed. Thus, they will feel themselves to
be the creators of their entire religion, and the most
intelligent among them will know how to draw the
required conclusions.

To weaken further the notion of "Real Presence" of Christ, all decorum will have to be set
aside. No more costly embroidered vestments; no
more sacred music, especially no more Gregorian
chant, but a music in jazz style; no more Sign of
the Cross; no more genuflections, but only dignified and stern attitudes.

Moreover the faithful will have to break themselves of the habit of kneeling, and this will be absolutely forbidden when receiving Communion.

Very soon, the Host will be laid in the hand in order that all notion of the Sacred be erased.

It will not be a bad thing to allow certain persons (previously chosen) to receive Communion under the two species, as priests do. . . because those who will not receive wine will become terribly jealous and therefore be tempted to abandon all religion (which is to be hoped for).

Besides, it will be strongly recommended not to say Mass anymore on weekdays; modern people have no time to lose. Another excellent method will consist in saying Mass at home, in the family, just before or after the meal taken in common. For this purpose, the fathers and mothers will be allowed to receive the Sacrament of Orders.

Who does not see the advantage of this method, which removes the need of costly places for the religion.

In order to destroy all sacredness in the worship, the priest will be invited to say the whole Mass in the vernacular and especially to recite the words of the Consecration as a narration—which they are in reality. He must not, above all, pronounce the following words: "This is my Body, this is my Blood," as if he really took the place of Christ who pronounced them.

Let everyone feel that the priest is reading a narration. Furthermore, there must never be question of a sacrifice, that is, a Mass-Sacrifice, a non-bloody renewal of the Sacrifice of the Cross. No Protestant accepts this phrase. Mass must only be a community meal for the greater welfare of human fraternity.

Moreover, when the Universal Church will be established, Mass will have no more reason to exist, except in families, I mean, the most fanatical ones.

We have to put up with this kind of people. But precisely by staying at home, they will become inoffensive. The prayers of the Ordinary of the Mass will be simplified to their maximum, and soon permission will be given to say but three prayers, that is, the Offertory, the Consecration and the Communion.

When we shall have succeeded in presenting different, simplified and humanized texts, it will be a good thing to recall, for the edification of the future generations, that there were some prayers of the Mass, called "of Saint Pius V," which greatly contributed to keeping the crowds in medieval obscurantism.

The following Offertory prayer is a model of its kind; it says: "Receive, O Holy Father, Almighty and Eternal God, this Spotless Host, which I, Thy unworthy servant, offer to Thee my living and true God, for my own countless sins, transgressions and negligences; for all here present and for all faithful Christians, living and dead, that it may avail both me and them unto salvation in everlasting life. Amen."

Who could say it better?

I suggest that all monasteries work on the composition of several Offertories and also of other prayers of the Mass. And, since the Offertory is an offering of bread, it seems sensible to me simply to say: "We bring here this bread made by the hand of man and which must serve as food for men."

Anyway, the words which tend to present this ceremony as sacred must be suppressed.

I will give only one example: In the old Mass, we have always said: "Jesus took bread in His Holy and Venerable hands". . .The word "Holy" must disappear from our vocabulary. We will not mention "Holy and Venerable Hands," we will say instead, "He took bread, blessed it," etc. . . .

This is a good example of the spirit with which this work must be pursued. For my part, I have not time at present, but later I will also compose one or more Masses of my own. On the other hand, this is a monk's work. Of course, when Mass will include only three obligatory prayers, it will always be permitted to add psalms, hymns, lectures and sermons...according to each one's taste.

Since this Mass will be only a common meal, it will be very important that this table be large enough to seat twelve persons.

I always thought it ridiculous that to eat, these people are obliged to inconvenience themselves and to rush out of their pews (one cannot deny that at the Communion table there is often a shuffle). It is their fault; why do they call a simple railing a "table"?

Therefore, I would like to see each church filled with tables, each one capable of seating twelve persons. Some believe that, at the Last Supper, there were thirteen, but since everybody is scared of that number, we will adopt the belief that Judas had gone out before the breaking of the bread. This will require ordaining a much larger number of priests. It is easy. It will be sufficient to require only a certain good will, a certain good conduct and no unending studies—no celibacy, of course. Nevertheless, those who wish to benefit by the strength brought about by continence will be monks or hermits, and those who wish to study will be theologians. There will be many kinds of priests. The usual one will be the married man, who will say Mass at home, at each meal. Since Mass will only be a "Lord's Supper," it will no longer be an act of adoration, but an act of fraternization.

It will not give thanks for illusory favors; it will not bring a forgiveness which it is unable to give; it will ask for nothing of the unknown mystery, but everything of man. . .

The Universal Church would therefore be entirely to the glory of man; it would exalt his greatness, his strength, his virility. It would offer incense to his rights and sing his victories.

# 15

## *How "Raven Hair" Writes A Letter Worthy Of Medieval And Romantic Obscurantism*

When I had finished my work on this first catechism, I received a long letter from "Raven Hair." An amazing letter, it said this:

"Darling:

"Thank you for the confidence which you have shown me and which incites me to open my heart completely to you. What does this heart say? That it loves you . . . and you know it . . . you know it only too well.

"It seems to me that your heart desires to have me share all your ideas, but I do not have this pretension; I only want to cry out to you, 'Beware, there lies a deathtrap!'

"Read, keep on reading. I pray you, do not get angry before you have read all my letter and have pondered on it. Surely, you think that you are right, as strongly as I do, but I tell you: read History again; the Church is immortal; you are wasting your time; you are wasting your strength. You cannot overpower God. If only you wanted to ponder on this: It is not because you do not believe in God that He does not exist.

"This ought to be easy for you to understand, because you believe it in the opposite sense. You imagine that God does not exist because I believe that He does. It is true that to believe or not to believe ultimately has no power at all.

"But, my Darling, all that lives around you proclaims the Presence of God. Have you made the seeds, have you made the laws? Is there a single blade of grass that is your work and therefore your property? Your own person does not belong to you. . .you did not ask to live and you possess nothing that you have not received.

"Even if you succeed in creating that strange Godless Church, you will not have won, because God would not be diminished by it. In no way can you diminish Him, nor of course, kill Him. I weep for you because you are engaged in this childish war. This God whom you wish to destroy is everywhere, Master of everything. By Him alone you live; by Him alone you keep on living. You might succeed in shaking His Church; this has happened many times during the last 2,000 years. . .but always it has revived more beautiful and stronger. The Church of Jesus Christ, Darling, has received the promise of Eternal Life; it knows and cries out to you by my mouth that the Holy Trinity will never abandon it and that all the attacks made against it are but trials which allow for purifying the Faith.

"Many souls, my Dear, will yield to the temptation of joining a completely human Church, which will mix up all beliefs so as to render them unrecognizable, but the Catholic Church will continue to stand. If you persecute it, it will go into hiding, but its soul will always remain standing. For the mark of this Church is the submission to a Revelation which comes from Heaven. Its particular domain is different from the one which you are accustomed to see. Its domain is Supernatural and Holy, so it matters not whether we are intelligent or not. My poor Darling, you are too intelligent. Moreover, you received a shock in your childhood. I do not ask you what kind. Have you not reached the age of looking upon the past with a serene soul? It seems to me that unconsciously you are seeking revenge. Is this a noble attitude? You were a very pious boy until you reached fourteen years of age, you told me, so that all my letter is asking you is to think—you know that. If you had been born in atheism, I would understand that you could not grasp that the domain of Faith belongs to another realm.

"I fear that your hatred for God and His Church

is the proof that you are not just a rebel, but a rebel who is a believer. It is said that they are the fiercest ones. I pity you with my whole heart, because you have lost in advance, and I am not scared, not at all. You might win a certain number of souls to your perverse doctrines, maybe even a part of the Clergy (although I do not believe it), but you will never win all the souls; on the contrary, you will fortify the Saints. Yes, my poor dear friend, by attacking the Church of God you are but a toy in the hands of the All-Powerful. You believe yourself to be strong, but you are only strong insofar as God permits. Fear the day when the Lord will say: 'It is enough, I have heard the prayers of those who suffer, and I have decided to comfort them by destroying My enemies.' God's enemy risks being His enemy for all Eternity, to his great despair, but it will be too late.

"You behave as if the Holy Church had no more power than a human institution, but we, we hold in our hands all that is needed to overthrow all the mountains of the world. But, by killing us, you will not destroy the forces which constitute our prerogative.

"When you are near me, when you are far away from me, Christ is between us two; I speak to Him, He looks at you, how He looks at you!

"How could it be otherwise, since I speak to Him about you, even in my dreams. You believe that you are free, that you are strong. What a mistake you make! Even if I had to die today, be very certain that I would continue to fight against your liberty—at least, against the use that you are making of it. I would marshal up the strength which you believe to represent the very strength of God.

"Do not smile, my big Darling; no, do not smile, but rather remember your childhood...you will see that you recognize very well this Invisible but so formidable Strength...but also so kind. My heart and my soul possess inexhaustible and indestructible powers; think about it calmly, remove from your mind all that your passion can dictate to you...do not willingly be deaf, nor willingly blind, it is not an attitude worthy of a man of heart...but you have turned your heart toward a love which is based on hatred, the hatred of God.

"Do you know that hatred is often the cry of a deceived love?

"As for me, I am sure that God loves you with a special love and that He is waiting for you with His customary patience. And since, at the present time, you do not want to pray to this God of Goodness, I am taking your place, and it is in your name that a thousand times a day I offer to the Allpowerful Lord the merits of His Son, those of the very holy Virgin Mary, of all the Saints known and unknown...I offer them with joy and confidence all day long and even during my sleep.

"You wish to transform the Mass and reduce it to a community meal...What a mockery! Masses—why we have already offered a few billion of them since the first Mass on Holy Thursday! Masses—why they go up as an incense of adoration at least one every second, and that throughout the whole day! I unite myself to these Adorable Sacrifices by which the Son again offers Himself for the salvation of mankind. I unite and offer myself to Him, I, who am so small . . . it seems that this offering is ridiculous, since I am so 'nothing' compared to Him. Of course, I am nothing . . . each one of us knows it perfectly well, and those who do not know it are to be pitied. There lies, I believe, the great difference between believers and unbelievers. Believers offer what they have received and which is immense; the others only desire to reign or to command or to discover or to dominate—or even to destroy.

"When I offer myself with Him at the Holy Sacrifice of the Mass, I thus offer all that He has given me; I give Him as a gift His own gifts and charities as a homage of gratitude . . .

"If you only knew all the loving interchanges which go on between Heaven and us . . . you would be crushed by fear, for you could then assess the mockery of your actions. I can only shed tears for you and these tears I offer as precious pearls. You have suffered and you have rebelled. If you had looked at a crucifix and if you had humbly prayed to the Lord to grant you His Peace and the strength to forgive, you would have felt such sweetness that spontaneously you would have thanked Him for the grief which had been graciously granted to you.

"Because this suffering was a beneficent gift, God was treating you as His beloved vineyard and was pruning you so that you could bear more fruit. (Is it not a fact that the vine never does prune itself?) But what fruit will the work bear which you have undertaken?. . . Fruits of bitterness, of solitude and of despair.

"Do you believe that I alone am fighting against you? No, my prayers are heard and transmitted by the immense assembly of those who have already reached Heaven.

"Do not smile, because the immortality of the soul is the only thing in yourself which you will never be able to destroy. The immortality of the soul. . . mark well these words, because they precisely mean that death does not exist. Every house should have these words engraved in golden letters on the walls of the sitting room. Instead of fearing death or of simply hating its notion, it should be known that death does not exist, and this is something infinitely more serious.

"Darling, I would prefer that you never loved me on this earth rather than to know that you are, for all Eternity, in that place where tears never dry. For I love you."

# 16

## *How The Sacrifice Of A Dear Friend Seems To Be Drowned In A Torrent Which Is About To Renovate The Face Of The Church*

I answered "Raven Hair's" letter by an increase in anti-apostolic zeal.

At that time, when we were nearing the end of this stupid war, I prepared a large number of attacks, for which I expected complete victory in a maximum of thirty years. I was musing about the year 1974, when I thought that I could celebrate the birth of a Universal Church without God.

My hatred for the Supernatural not only gave me genius, but also unbelievable strength for my double work. For let us not forget, I was studying theology, and it was very important that I should get good grades. In fact, I was the best in every-thing, which caused me to laugh and strength-ened me in my conviction that a God who did not take pains to defend his true faithful did not exist.

The word "supernatural" conceals all that man does not understand behind changing curtains, moved by fanciful delusions. I decided to destroy this bad theater. I entrusted to my correspondents the task of expurgating the New Testament of everything which was not perfectly natural and explainable. This work is quite useful, since Christ Himself believed in His own Divinity, at least if we accept what some pretend that He said. But since it is impossible to distinguish between what He really said and what the Evangelists have added, we must refuse to admit altogether all that is repugnant to common sense.

As I have already said, the most virile action is the one which attacks the problem of children and exerts a strong influence on their feeble minds. With the most ardent conviction, I sent orders concerning the liberty of each individual, liberty which must be granted to every child as soon as it can walk and speak. It is shameful, truly and terribly shameful, that parents oblige their children to go to Mass every Sunday. It is not less shameful that they register them for catechism classes without asking them their advice.

It follows from this that these poor little ones believe themselves obliged to receive Communion, even when they prefer to go out to play. What more

can we say about Baptism, which is conferred on
them at their very birth!!! There starts the real scandal. I suggested an energetic campaign of information for youth.

Let everybody devote himself, at church, at catechism classes, at school, on the radio, in order that
all the children of the world be informed of their
absolute right to say "No" to their parents, when
they want to make them become obedient and
hypocritical little Christians.

A happy day it will be when thousands of children will say openly and joyfully: "I am not a Christian. I do not believe in God. I am not so naive
as my parents, who are old and good for nothing."

On the other hand, I had a burning desire to
see "Raven Hair" again, and this desire was ful-
filled without my having humbly to request it.

I received a charming word of invitation, telling me that she wanted to present me a request.

On a Saturday, when the sun was shining very
brightly, I charged at top speed into the shop where
"Raven Hair" was waiting for me. Who will ever
be able to understand the meaning for me of those
ordinary words: " 'Raven Hair' is waiting for me"?

"Raven Hair" was so completely mine that I
would have liked to cut her hair so that no one

else could see it. Cut it! What a criminal idea had come into my mind!

She was all sweetness and love when she told me that she had a request to make. I almost trembled. But all that she wanted was simply to draw my hands which are, they say, admirable. Truly, women have some absurd, though charming ideas.

I posed, therefore, for the whole afternoon with a patience that the angels would envy me for, if they existed, and this solely for my hands.

Sketches were quickly drawn, one after the other, on the floor, and I was floating in a sort of ecstasy, which must be called perfect happiness, I suppose. . .at least, since then, I do not recall having felt one so grand.

I know that no one will believe it, but our union was so strong and perfect during those hours that I doubt whether the trivial carnal union can cause such a happiness, which seemed to elude time. When enough sketches had been made, my charming enemy explained to me that they were certainly destined to perform great things. I was almost embarrassed, because the truth was that my hands seemed to have a liking for death and murder.

It was on that same day that she allowed me to undo her hair and to play with it. I tried different hairdos, I braided it, I rolled it, then I brushed it with great care, as if I would never see it again, as if I was preparing it for a painful sacrifice. Why did I have such a strange feeling on that day? But the whole day was truly strange. Even today, I cannot explain whence came those mysterious feelings.

We separated with tragic difficulty. "Will see you next Saturday." "Next Saturday," we both said, as if this hope were to be written in a prophetic memory, as if we would find in it our only basis for good-bye, as if we wanted to overthrow in advance all obstacles. . .Overthrow obstacles!!! And I who had completely forgotten that on that Saturday we would begin our retreat, we who would receive Orders in only a few days.

I therefore had to write a short letter to "Raven Hair" and invent a plausible lie. I would have liked to add in all simplicity that I would soon go to Rome and that I hoped that she would follow me there.

But how can I talk of simplicity when everything in me cried out that I was entering a slavery much worse than the one which I had suffered during these six years of seminary?

In Rome, I would be caught in the gears of the Eternal City; I would be caught, but I would console myself, remembering that I was the particle of sand which must jam the machine—jam it so well that it could never be repaired.

I therefore started my retreat to prepare myself for the last ceremony, which would make me a priest for eternity.

Since I do not believe in eternity, I did not suffer by this prospect. It was just a bad moment to go through, as at the dentist's, when there for a good reason.

The important thing is to have faith, and mine was worth theirs. What am I saying? Mine surpassed theirs, because it was not childish, filled with scares and terrors. The great day arrived at last, as journalists say. I was calm. Many tried to make up for my absent family. Each one rivaled the other in kindness. A nice little scuffle would have done me more good, but it is difficult to want to be a half supernatural being and at the same time claim the right to hit a few enemies, even fictitious ones.

When I entered the chapel, I was perfectly modest and humble. These virtues are an easy game to play, when a secret pride and a higher aim support them.

I was walking with a gliding step, eyes lowered, when a stifled cry, exclamations and a real disorder were heard on my left. Normally, I should not have looked. But I disobeyed my conscience (I mean the one which they had created for me and which I manipulated with amusement).

I saw young men lifting a fainted girl. Her man-
tilla had fallen and her long black hair was dissar-
ranged and was dragging on the floor of the chapel.
When I lifted my eyes to turn them away from this
scene, I met the keen look of the professor who
had acted as my mailbox.

What was he doing there? Was he the one who
had brought "Raven Hair?"

During this short exchange of looks, I thought
that I read in this man the expression of a cruel
triumph.

I promised myself that I would discover the
truth and that I would make whomever had com-
mitted this infamy pay dearly for it. The rest of
the day, therefore, passed in a sorrowful mist. Each
one could surmise all kinds of doubts about me,
but I did not care. I did not even have any more
desire to seem honorably pious and to hear soft
voices prophesy my future holiness.

Happily, the student came to greet me. He was
my only friend. I told him briefly what had happened and I asked him to make an inquiry. I wanted
to know, I wanted to kill, I wanted to cry out, to
defend myself, to defend her—especially to defend
her—but it was too late, forever too late. If only
I had the courage to tell her all by myself, she might
have accepted suffering in silence and loving me
secretly.

During the following days, I prepared my trip to the U.S.A., where I wanted to visit the most important Protestant sects in order to find out how to control them. Until then, forcibly, I had been obliged to neglect too much the important factor of faith, so solidly anchored in the Protestant world. It was imperative that I should know well this aspect of the problem before going on to continue my studies in Rome. Just before my departure, the student came running to tell me the news which would make me suffer the most: the entrance of "Raven Hair" into a Carmelite monastery. She was there for my sake; never anymore would she have the least lover's joy. . .for my sake. I do not know if I would not have preferred to see her die. Anyway, I swore to myself that I would have all the monasteries of the world opened and in particular the contemplative monasteries. I launched a very ardent campaign against gratings, and I even had requests sent to the Pope, through very naive nuns.

I reminded them that gratings had been necessary to keep unwilling young girls from escaping who had been forced to enter by their parents. It was to prevent them from running away and from corresponding that these gratings were double and reinforced by wooden shutters. I did all that I could to obtain that this vestige of so-called divine imprisonment be abolished. I invoked, above all, the sense of honor of these consecrated virgins, in order that they might foster the holy desire to remain freely cloistered in houses open to all. Later, I went much further, by imploring the nuns to return to the world, which needed their presence very much. I even persuaded them that they would do more good by not showing, by a special dress, what they were.

There were writers keen enough to write whole books on this subject, with a luxury of vocabulary truly admirable. I also fought tooth and nail against the custom of shaving the heads of cloistered nuns. I contended that their shaved heads rendered them ridiculous when they had to go to a clinic to undergo some operation. I insisted on the young vocations which were stupidly lost on account of these customs of another age. I attacked the old and solemn costumes, so heavy in summer and not very efficient against cold in winter. I suggested that all the rules and constitutions be carefully revised, preferably by men (in their generosity, women have a certain tendency toward exaggeration).

But, when I beheld the great extension of my work, I stumbled on a silent obstacle, although so small in the face of the Cosmos...a modest and very secret Carmelite monastery from which I never received a single letter. On the one side, there was the world; on the other, this jail. I had command over the first, but I was a prisoner of the other.

Nevertheless, my work did not suffer from this—on the contrary.

Paradoxically, I almost boiled with rage when I considered the uselessness of "Raven Hair's" sacrifice, a sacrifice so total and vain!

My work was functioning at a rather monotonous pace when rumors concerning the possible opening of a Universal Council came to stimulate my zeal. I learned that some schemas were being prepared by order of the Pope. I convinced my superiors that maybe a definitive role could be played. I was then appointed to the highest post. Everything depended on me, and my funds were practically unlimited.

I financed leftist reviews and also a large number of journalists, who performed excellent work afterwards. All my hopes laid principally on alternate schemas, which I had suggested through much-advanced and audacious theologians.

I think that ambition guided them; it is the most powerful of driving forces. I succeeded in obtaining copies of all the official schemas, I mean, those commanded by the Pope. They were, for me, catastrophic, absolutely calamitous, and I weigh my words. Even at this very hour, many years after the end of the Council, I still shudder with cold (a stupid expression which I use through laziness).

Suppose that these schemas were edited and widely circulated, and all my work would be set back to zero (or almost). Finally, thanks to my zeal and especially to the money which I spent as if it were inexhaustible, the modernist schemas (oh, very timidly modernist, I must confess) were brought in secretly to the Council and presented with audacity to replace the official ones, about which they complained for not having been worked out in full liberty, the holy liberty of the children of God (as they say).

This sleight-of-hand trick filled the whole Assembly with such stupefaction that they have not yet gotten over it and will never be able to—which proves that audacity always pays. Is it not what Danton has said?

———————

Nevertheless, I am not satisfied. No, this Council was not what I was hoping for. We will have to wait for Vatican III. There we will gain a complete victory. As for Vatican II, I do not know what happened. It seemed as if an invisible devil would stop all our efforts of modernization, just at the moment they would have become efficacious. Strange and maddening!

———————

Happily, since then we have found the astuteness—which consists in hiding behind the "Spirit of the Council"—to launch all kinds of thrilling innovations. This expression, "Spirit of the

Council," has become for me a master-trump. As for me, it is like playing a game of cards. I cut and over-cut, or I play the master-trump, which enables me to pick up the last little hearts, the small non-silvery clubs and the disarmed little spades. But it will be only at Vatican III that I will be able to present myself with hammer and nails, not to nail God on His Cross, but rather to nail Him in His coffin.

## THE END

*The briefcase contained no schemas concerning Vatican III, and yet it is very probable that such texts do exist and are studied, compared, made worse... In a small notebook, a few notes in Russian, which I had discreetly translated, also gave me brief indications about the future projects of my wounded man.*

*For people like Michael, Vatican II was only a trial-balloon which history will hardly mention. But Vatican III will seal the alliance of Christianity and Marxism, and the most remarkable change will be the plurality of religious dogmas and the uncompromising character of social dogmas.*

*All religions, Christian or not, forming but one vast Association, will be reduced to their common denominator, "magic," and will give to the subconscious (at least to the more crafty) a real power controlled by the "Pure" (read, "Marxist").*

---

*The surprising thing is that nobody ever came to claim Michael's papers, at least, not until today. But he had bought his car under a false name and probably neglected to inform anyone of his trip.*

*I do not know where "Raven Hair" is. Maybe she is still in a Carmelite Monastery in which the prioress must have maintained the Faith of older days. Maybe this book will someday discreetly penetrate into that Carmelite Monastery, that "Raven Hair" might know that I also pray for Michael.*

# Comments from Readers

The author, Marie Carré, has received many approbations; here are the most characteristic:

- "The case presented in this book is not an imaginary one, alas; if my memory is correct, it is in a recent 'Bulletin of Aid to the Church in Need,' that a specialist of problems behind the Iron Curtain asserts that Bishop "N" is in fact an agent...and that he is the one who had 10,000 churches closed in Russia."
- "I congratulate you for having uncovered the core of the 'devilish system' which so few know and for having expounded it, not as an abstract professor, but on the march, so to speak, and in 'effervescence,' in a man possessed by the Devil."
- "The story is poignant, and I believe that it rests on a basis of reality. I am convinced that there are in the Church, among the priests and maybe the bishops, some people who have been of the AA."
- "I was asking myself if this little book would have some influence on our countrymen, who read very little. Yes indeed, true Christians are familiar with the Gospel texts in which there is very little abstract theology and many stories. And all of theology is contained there. They understand *AA-1025.*"

These manuscript texts, perfectly authentic, come from correspondents whose names will not be divulged because they belong to the personal correspondance of the author.                —The Editor

"Three times I have read *AA-1025*, written by Marie Carré. I believe it my duty to invite all Catholics to read this book, if they wish to understand clearly what the Holy Father, Pope Paul VI, wishes to say when he puts Catholics on guard against the auto-demolition of the Church, that is to say, its destruction from within."

—Mgr. Ira Bourassa
Therbrooke, Quebec, Canada

"The book of Marie Carré, *AA-1025*, is a poignant document. It deserves to be spread, for it will open the eyes of the faithful to the diabolical plots of the Communists. I have ordered a dozen copies to pass out."

—Can. Georges Panneton,
Three Rivers, Quebec, Canada

"If one wishes to know the tactics employed by the Communist Party to infiltrate and subvert the Catholic Church from within, one must read *AA-1025*. It is a tale of a diabolical adventure which catches at one's throat, not to organize a 'Witch hunt,' but to be informed before it is too late."

—Joseph d'Anjou, S.J.,
14, Dauphine St., Quebec, Canada

"The fantastic plan to turn the Church into an instrument of Communist conquest would be unbelievable if we were not every day witnesses of its realization."

—Henry MacFarland

# ORDER FORM

## Quantity Discount

| | | |
|---|---|---|
| 1 | 7.50 each | |
| 5 | 4.00 each | 20.00 total |
| 10 | 3.50 each | 35.00 total |
| 25 | 3.00 each | 75.00 total |
| 100 | 2.50 each | 250.00 total |

*Prices subject to change.*

Gentlemen:

Please send me _____ copy(ies) of **AA-1025**.

☐ Enclosed is my payment of _____.

☐ Please bill my

    ☐ VISA  ☐ MasterCard  ☐ Discover Card

    in the amount of _____.

My Card No. is _____Exp. Date _____

Tel. no. _____Email _____

Name _____

Street _____

City _____

State _____ Zip _____

U.S. & CAN. POST/HDLG: If total order=$1-$10, add $3.00;
$10.01-$25, add $5.00; $25.01-$50, add $6.00;
$50.01-$75, add $7.00; $75.01-$150, add $8.00;
orders of $150.01 or more, add $10.00.

**TAN BOOKS AND PUBLISHERS, INC.**
**P.O. Box 424**
**Rockford, Illinois 61105**
**1-800-437-5876**               **www.tanbooks.com**